Step Up

How to Advocate Like a Woman

Ellen Troxclair

Published by Authorsunite.com

To my family, who are my world,
and the dedicated volunteers who made my
election possible.

CONTENTS

PART ONE

THE CHALLENGE

1

The Unlikely Candidate

It seems like everyone else has it all together, doesn't it? Whether we're comparing ourselves to the rose-colored view of other people's lives on social media or a TV drama, it's hard to feel like we're living up to expectations.

In reality, I *do* have it all, but it looks a lot different from what you see on TV and comes with more sacrifice and hard work than my Instagram feed would have you believe.

My husband, Caleb, and I have a loving and supportive marriage, but every day is a new challenge as we figure out the best way to raise our three young children together. We're both self-employed, and with the flexibility of managing our own schedules comes the uncertainty of fluctuating income and never really having any time "off." In addition to marriage and parenting, I'm balancing running a real estate business with dedicating significant time toward my passion: being an advocate for my community through political and non-profit work.

Juggling these responsibilities isn't easy, but it's no different than millions of American women across the country. (Current status: rocking a newborn to sleep in one arm, his head perched in the bend of my elbow, while slowly typing one-handed with the other.)

I always manage to make it work, but oh my gosh, I'm tired. And that's with serious help with childcare, house tidying, and scheduling. After having three babies in three years, I'm thrilled to enjoy a guilt-free glass of wine (can I get a hallelujah!), but I'm often too tired to finish it.

It's hard to believe that five short years ago, I was a 29-year-old newlywed who was frustrated and fed up with the misguided direction of our city. I made the life-changing decision to run for the Austin City Council - and won.

Now, I've completed a four-year term serving as the only conservative on an increasingly leftist city council. I fought to lower property taxes and spend taxpayer money efficiently and effectively, and I served as an unwavering advocate for accountable government. I provided tangible property tax relief to homeowners, piloted a program to give panhandlers the dignity of work, and made sure that kids could sell lemonade in their front yard without first seeking a permit from the health department. I served a city of nearly one million people, with a staff of over 13,000, and an annual budget of $4 billion.

I found myself as the critical vote in the middle of a ridesharing saga that made national news, and despite my efforts otherwise, ultimately pushed Uber and Lyft out of Austin. Shortly thereafter, I successfully advocated at the state level for their return (more on this later). As the only council member to also hold a job outside of the full-time elected office, I continued to manage my residential real estate business, allowing me to hear from people in the "real world" about how the decisions being made in city hall were negatively impacting their families.

I was a lightning rod for the liberal establishment, which often tried to silence and demean me. I struggled not to let the belittlement from my detractors outweigh the loyal support from so many others. I had crushing defeats and often wondered whether it was worth it (it was). I had days of jubilation, knowing that initiatives that I advocated for, and passed, improved our community, and that I was following through on my campaign promises.

I had two babies while in office, and a third shortly thereafter, balancing the demands of pregnancy and newborns (and the sleep deprivation that accompanies them) with the responsibilities of the job.

It is all still a little surreal to me. I was no different or more qualified than so many other women who approach the challenges of work and family with tenacity and grace. I just happened to step outside my comfort zone and put my name on the ballot to run for office. And this one decision has given me a platform to speak up for people and communities who were otherwise unrepresented and the ability to affect policy changes that reached well beyond my district.

Time to Step Up

Jeanette Rankin was the first woman elected to the United States Congress in 1916. The Republican from Montana foretold, "I may be the first woman member of Congress, but I won't be the last."

The Nineteenth Amendment to the United States Constitution was adopted a few years later in 1920, giving women the right to vote.

In 100 years since that historic change, progress in electing women has been slow. Out of 11,000 people who have been elected to Congress, only 318 women have ever been elected to the House, and only 56 women have ever made it the Senate.[1] Five states have never sent a woman to represent them in the U.S. House, and 21 states have never been represented by a female in the Senate.[2]

> Out of 11,000 people who have been elected to Congress, only 318 women have ever been elected to the House, and only 56 women have ever made it the Senate. Five states have never sent a woman to represent them in the U.S. House, and 21 states have never been represented by a woman in the Senate.

According to She Should Run, there are 500,000 total elected offices in the country. Less than one-third are held by women. In 23 states, no woman has ever been elected governor. In 7 states, women comprise less than 20% of the legislature.[3]

While the first female Congresswoman may have been Republican, Democrat women greatly outnumber Republican women serving at the national level. Congress has 106 Democrat women compared to only 21 Republican women. As of 2019, twice as many Democrat women as Republican women are serving in elected office at the state level.

The disparity in women's voices between the two parties is alarming. While more women serving in office should be celebrated regardless of party affiliation, the statistics are a wake-up call for women who lean right of center.

When women run, we win at the same rate as men! So, it's not that we're not winning, it's that we're not running. By failing to put

When women run, we win at the same rate as men! So, it's not that we're not winning, it's that we're not running.

ourselves on the ballot, we are sabotaging the efforts to further the beliefs we care about, missing the opportunity to be effective messengers to independent voters, and leaving the next generation without the role models they need to see in elected office.

History is filled with examples of women who cared enough to take action in their local communities and make the world around them a better place. Sometimes all it takes is bravery and willingness to step outside your comfort zone to make a change for the better.

President Theodore Roosevelt once said: *"Do what you can, with what you have, where you are."* He was on to something. Regardless of how much time you have and what resources are available, you can always do something to make a difference.

The cause could be school choice for children, lowering taxes, or even something as simple as providing for a local family in need. It could be traffic solutions, reducing barriers for small businesses, or advocating for parks. It could be supporting police and fire departments, revitalizing an underserved area, or streamlining human services programs. It doesn't matter what that cause is, as long as it is something you have a desire to impact.

I hope this book will serve as inspiration, spurring women to bring the same leadership, compassion, and tenacity that they already provide for their families and communities into advocacy for our republic.

While we could benefit from more representation from women on both sides of the aisle, the statistics are clear - we need more right-of-center women to step up to balance our policy conversations and accurately represent the makeup of our country. I've written this book specifically with those women in mind.

Women who consider themselves Republicans, conservatives, Libertarians, Independents, and everything in between are being drowned out or completely ignored in today's political battles. The Left has succeeded in owning the narrative surrounding so-called "women's issues," despite not representing a huge swath of women in America. The fate of our country is at a tipping point, and too many conservative women are sitting on the sidelines.

In addition to the lessons learned from my experience in elected office and how I came to be there, you'll come away understanding why your voice is so important and be armed with a playbook on how to be heard.

Prior to writing this, I set out to see if other female leaders from across the country had similar experiences in an effort to identify common barriers and strategies for success. What I found was shockingly consistent - women face a confidence gap that causes them to be less likely to find themselves in positions of influence in policy and politics. They need to be encouraged repeatedly by others to step outside their comfort zones, but once they do, they overcome unfounded fears to provide dynamic, inspiring, and desperately needed leadership to our communities and country.

You'll be inspired by people such as Patricia Rucker, the Venezuelan immigrant who was a homeschool mom of five before being elected to her state senate, Congresswoman McMorris Rodgers, one of the highest-ranking Republican women in Congress, and many other compelling leaders who share their stories.

You'll be better prepared to identify - and overcome - the personal and professional barriers that often hold conservative women back from stepping up in a more public way. Most of all, you'll be determined to take the next step in your own journey of being a part of the change you want to see in your community and your country.

Whether it is joining an organization, volunteering for a political campaign, or running for office, we need more women to get off the sidelines and onto the playing field. Too much is at stake. For the sake of our families and our communities, we need YOU to STEP UP and impact the direction of our nation's future.

The Unlikely Candidate

My memory of Election Day is simultaneously vivid and a blur. For over twelve hours, I spent every minute talking with shoppers as they walked from their cars into the grocery store, which also happened to serve as the biggest polling location in the city council district I sought to represent.

Standing in my campaign "uniform," made up of a worn navy-blue t-shirt with my campaign logo on it and a pair of jeans, I quickly explained to hurried voters why I was running and asked them to cast their ballot for me. By the time the polls had closed, it was dark, cold, and pouring down rain. I slumped, exhausted, into the driver's seat of my car with no idea what the night would hold.

I did know that, win or lose, I had put everything I possibly could into my campaign. We had knocked on thousands of doors, made even more phone calls, raised every dollar possible, and stood in this parking lot for the entire two weeks of early voting earning every last vote.

We ran the best race we could, for the right reasons, and the result was in God's hands now.

I was the underdog from the beginning: a 29-year-old woman who had no previous experience in elected office. But I channeled my frustration into an intense and passionate campaign. I had left it all on the field, and despite not knowing how the results would play out, a serene sense of peace washed over me as I drove away.

As I changed out of my campaign t-shirt and into a sweater and black pants for the election night watch party, it occurred to me that depending on the results, this may be the last time I would ever wear that shirt. My feet were sore, and I was tempted to hide out in my room and temper my hopes, bracing myself for what could be a disappointing evening. But there were friends and family waiting on me, and I summoned the last bit of adrenaline I had. On my way to join supporters at the party, I couldn't help but marvel at how I had found myself in this situation.

It was happenstance that I was distracted in class one day while pursuing a business degree at the University of Texas when I came across a job posting from a state representative who was looking for an intern to help in his Capitol office during the next legislative session. It seemed like an interesting opportunity to learn firsthand how government really worked.

What initially started as a curiosity soon led to a full-on fascination. I quickly fell in love with public policy - seeing how, and why, new laws were created - and knowing that I could have an impact on making the state a better place. As a result, I ended up spending much of my twenties working in the Texas House of Representatives. The pay was low, but the work was fulfilling.

The best part was being able to solve problems behind the scenes without the pressure of living under the limelight. I had the utmost respect for the men and women who had the courage to put their name on the ballot and run for office, but the idea of being under a microscope and subjecting myself to scrutiny and criticism was not particularly appealing. The amount of public speaking that being a candidate and elected official demanded was even more terrifying. Definitely not for me!

As fate would have it, these were fears that I would eventually have to face.

Governor Rick Perry once described Austin, Texas as "the blueberry in the tomato soup."

The analogy made sense for good reason. The Democrats have not elected one of their candidates to statewide office since George W. Bush won the governorship in 1994. Meanwhile, the Austin City Council has consisted almost exclusively of left-leaning elected officials for decades.

For years, conservatives had written off Austin's local government as a lost cause, much like national Democrats had written off Texas.

Prior to my campaign for city council, Austin was the largest city in the nation with at-large districts, rather than council members who represented the geographic area in which they lived. As a result, a small concentration of political activists downtown maintained complete control over our local government and largely left minorities, conservatives, and suburbanites feeling underrepresented.

This all changed in 2012 when Austin voters approved a new system, which put in place ten single-member districts across the city. Now, council members would be directly accountable to constituents in their district, not to a small minority of political activists from other parts of the city.

For the first time, we had a chance to elect a few reasonable, fiscally conservative members to stand up to the status quo and represent a different viewpoint. The possibility was thrilling. If we could move the needle just a few degrees to the right, we had a better chance of reining in the skyrocketing cost-of-living, excessive spending, and growing property tax bills.

Our city was at a tipping point, and the decisions being made at city hall were pushing us closer and closer to the edge. The people who made Austin so unique were being forced out of the city, no longer able to afford the cost of a ballooning, inefficient local government.

But as we moved closer and closer to the filing deadline to run for office, it became increasingly clear that none of the declared candidates shared my values or would be willing to put up the fight necessary to solve the systemic issues that plagued our city.

Despite the unprecedented chance to elect some commonsense, like-minded leaders, my husband, Caleb, and I were disappointed that we were going to be stuck with more of the same. I didn't know much about city politics, but I knew that we were heading in the wrong direction. I also knew it was a shame to waste this unique opportunity.

Refusing to accept this reality, I woke up one morning with a crazy idea.

I looked over and said to my husband, "What if I ran for city council?"

Confused, he replied, "But, don't you hate public speaking?"

He was right. I was a truly terrible public speaker and had never expressed any desire to run for office until that morning. There were a million other reasons not to - we didn't know the right people, we couldn't self-fund a campaign, and I would have to quit a job that I loved if I won. But I realized that if I had the ability to run and chose not to, I had no right to complain about the representation I was given. It was time for me to step up or shut up.

> If I had the ability to run and chose not to, I had no right to complain about the representation I was given.

The more we talked about the idea, the more serious I became. With an important filing deadline approaching, we were up against the clock to make a decision. We talked over the challenges that taking on this endeavor would pose, along with why we believed it was so important. We calculated estimates of what it would cost to run an impactful campaign and the difficulties of raising money. I got the okay from my boss, Representative Jason Isaac, who was wholeheartedly supportive. I was nervous, but the encouragement from those around me gave me the courage to move forward. I filed the necessary paperwork to run for office, and there was no turning back.

After I joined the race, the total number of candidates came to five. I immediately began receiving requests to participate in candidate forums and speak at local political clubs and neighborhood organizations. And I needed to raise money fast if I was going to be a viable candidate. It was a whirlwind.

I dreaded the first debate and the public speaking it would entail. The idea of calling strangers and asking them to help fund my campaign was uncomfortable. But I knew this was what it would take if I wanted to serve as a commonsense voice for our community. I was far from polished, but by speaking from my heart, people could sense I was running for the right reasons and that my passion was genuine.

Along with some amazing volunteers who were beside me every step of the way, I spent months knocking on doors, making phone calls, hosting events, and visiting with the constituents I was seeking to represent. The district had nearly 100,000 people, and I wanted to reach as many of them as possible. I talked about skyrocketing property taxes, and my ideas to help provide relief, every chance I could.

I was pretty sure my message was resonating with voters because my small but dedicated army of volunteers was growing every week, and my yard signs were popping up all over the district. However, it wasn't until after the annual property tax bills arrived in mailboxes that I knew for sure this was the message that could win this election.

Social media and news outlets were ablaze with angry residents who were upset about yet another huge increase in their tax bills. The increases were outpacing people's ability to pay, and they were fed up. It must have been obvious to my opponents as well, because every other candidate suddenly began talking about this issue. Unfortunately for them, I already owned the message.

Because we were running in a nonpartisan race, there was no primary. With five people in an election that required a majority to win, it was a near certainty that there would be a runoff between the top two vote-getters. The general election was just the first hurdle. The goal was to make the runoff and continue the fight from there.

I made sure my campaign maintained meticulous data of every supportive voter we came in contact with and what their concerns were, so we knew exactly whom we needed to get back out to the polls if I made the runoff. Winning the first election would only get me to the finals. We would need to turn voters out a second time to get across the finish line.

The election took place in November in a non-presidential year, and Election Day was quickly approaching. In the home stretch, I spent my time at high-profile voting locations, making one last pitch for my candidacy as voters entered the polls. Before I knew it, Election Day was here and then over, and the final votes had been cast.

Once the polls were closed, I reminded myself of what former President John Quincy Adams said: "Duty is ours, results are God's."

As the evening wore on, the results finally trickled in. In a moment of shock and amazement, I realized that I, the underdog, had not just made the runoff, but was leading the field. I had hoped to take the second-place spot and was optimistic about my chances, but I did not dream that I would earn the most votes to beat out all other challengers. I was headed to a runoff against the second-place finisher. We celebrated that evening, knowing that the next morning would present a new challenge.

I was relieved, but also bracing myself for another six weeks of campaigning. There was a lot of work to do if we were going to be successful in the runoff. I had to simultaneously activate my base and ensure they returned to vote, while convincing a lot of fiscally conservative Democrats to vote for me as well. It is common for the second-place finisher in a general election to end up winning the runoff. They often work harder to overcome their deficit and collect voters from the unsuccessful candidates. I didn't want to find myself in that situation.

The runoff was an exhausting sprint, working every day to get supporters back out to the polls for the December runoff, knowing that the race would likely be decided by a handful of votes. I spent another week in that same grocery store parking lot as Election Day, part 2, approached.

After the polls closed, I was inundated with text messages.

"Congrats!" one of the messages said.

"On what?" I wrote back.

"Early voting numbers are in, and you are in the lead," they replied.

I had a head start, but a lot of votes still needed to be counted. At the election night watch party, the clock seemed frozen, and it was difficult mingling with people as I repeatedly refreshed the browser on my phone to see if the final results had been tallied. My lead narrowed as the night wore on, and I wondered nervously if I was going to be able to hang on. While it felt like the results would never come in, a few hours later the race was called: I had won - by just 57 votes.

"This election just goes to show you that your vote really does matter. Your voice really does count," I told the friends and supporters who were gathered. "It is your job to hold me accountable to my campaign promises. You have my cell phone number - please use it."

This is how I found my 29-year-old self serving as the youngest woman ever elected to the Austin City Council, the 11th-largest city in the country.

I was not the perfect candidate. I had to put on a bold front and fake it until I made it.

I had doubts about my ability to win. I certainly had doubts about my ability to be an effective spokesperson. Thank goodness I did not allow them to derail the opportunity to be an impactful leader.

There is no perfect time to run for office. Had I waited until I felt like I was polished and prepared, that time would never have come, and the opportunity would have long passed. As it turns out, it was the ideal time to run, I was the right candidate, and I could be a compelling advocate.

KEY INSIGHTS

- **2020 marks the 100-year anniversary since women earned the right to vote, but women are still shockingly behind when it comes to representation in elected offices.**
- **Female Democrats in office far outnumber female Republicans. There is a need and opportunity for right-of-center women to step up.**
- **"Do what you can, with what you have, where you are."**

CALL TO ACTION

Read on to be inspired by women who are making a difference. Then follow the comprehensive guide on how you can, too.

2

Are you a Feminist?

Have you ever been asked if you're a feminist? If so, how did you answer?

For me and many other women, it is a question that is almost impossible to answer with a simple yes or no.

I recently posed this question to a group of friends and each had a different answer that involved some sort of qualification, like "Yes, but . . ." or "No, because . . ."

When I'm asked this question, I end up feeling like I have to apologize for not identifying as a feminist. How did this happen?

Webster's Dictionary defines feminism as "the theory of the political, economic, and social equality of the sexes."[4] Under that definition, what woman, or man for that matter, wouldn't consider themselves a feminist?

Unfortunately, over the years, feminism has warped into a leftist advocacy movement that has nothing to do with ensuring equality for all, and everything to do with undermining and discrediting any woman who disagrees with the current leftist causes.

Conservative pundit Laura Ingraham underscores this point quite eloquently: *I don't think there is a 'woman's view.' Women are people. They have different views on a whole range of subjects. But if you watched television, every time someone said, 'From the women's point of view,' it was always a liberal.*[5]

It is ridiculous that fewer than half of all women determine what are considered acceptable beliefs for all of womankind. It is even more ludicrous that many of these beliefs include policies that directly undermine women.

We need to step up and take this movement back. Or better yet, create a new movement that acknowledges our strength, intelligence, and independence. A movement that inspires us to be involved in politics and public policy, while remaining inclusive to women from all walks of life. A movement that doesn't judge women who choose their families over their careers and stands by a woman's right to hold a variety of different viewpoints, including positions that are fiscally and socially conservative.

The "Women's" March

The need for a movement like this has perhaps never been more evident than after the Women's March, where thousands of women gathered in Washington D.C. and around the nation to protest the day after President Donald Trump's inauguration in January 2017.

Organizers claimed the protest was to *"stand together in solidarity with our partners and children for the protection of our rights, our safety, our health, and our families."*[6]

Support for protecting our rights, health, safety, and families is virtually universal for both men and women. Unfortunately, the Women's March had little to do with improving the quality of life for women and their families, and everything to do with protesting the election of the President.

Their mission statement wasn't an authentic call for unity, but a thinly veiled attempt to seize on the President's contentious rhetoric to advocate for controversial social issues such as abortion.

This is a shame, because a lot of good could be done through women uniting around common issues. While the Women's March prides itself on diversity of race and sexual orientation, it does not seem to have the same respect for celebrating diversity of opinion.

The most recent Gallup Poll shows that only 50% of women identify as pro-choice nationwide.[7] Despite this fact, abortion has become a litmus test. If you are not pro-choice, you are considered anti-women and thus should not even have a seat at the table or be part of the debate - even if you are a woman.

By making abortion its central issue, the Women's March has alienated nearly half of our country's women from joining the conversation and getting involved. Pigeonholing women and allowing so-called "women's issues" to be synonymous with abortion and birth control has diminished women's voices on issues that impact our lives every day such as tax policy, national security, and education.

> Pigeonholing women and allowing so-called "women's issues" to be synonymous with abortion and birth control has diminished women's voices on issues that impact our lives every day such as tax policy, national security, and education.

Carrie Lukas, President of the Independent Women's Forum, showcased the lack of input conservative women have on the feminist movement in a Forbes op-ed:

"Glamour Magazine's 2019 college women of the year checked every box on progressive's diversity list. Each woman was undeniably impressive and accomplished. But it was no accident that they also represented an array of ethnicities and were advancing abortion rights, gun control, climate change solutions, and a political platform similar to Alexandria Ocasia-Cortez's.

One sizable minority group . . . was left completely out: Women who identify as conservative."[8]

Why have we allowed a small vocal minority to hijack the role of women in politics? If you only pay attention to the mainstream media, you would believe that all women spend their Saturdays protesting restrictions on abortion while wearing pink "pussy hats."

This type of "activism" is the last thing on the minds of the women I know.

The women I know spend their time balancing the needs of their careers, families, and community. They are active in their churches, non-profit causes, and local schools and care deeply for the world around them. Yet, many are hesitant to speak up about politics because they are afraid they will be villainized for having opinions out of sync with the media's caricature of what women should believe.

> The women I know spend their time balancing the needs of their careers, families, and community. They are active in their churches, non-profit causes, and local schools and care deeply for the world around them. Yet, many are hesitant to speak up about politics because they are afraid they will be villainized for having opinions out of sync with the media's caricature of what women should believe.

The climate has become significantly more hostile toward conservative women in recent years, so it is easy to understand why center-right women are afraid to speak up and get involved in the political process. Just look at how public figures and the media treat women who do.

Alexis Grenell stated in a *New York Times* editorial that women who do not follow the status quo on women's issues are "gender traitors" who make "standing by the patriarchy a full-time job."[9] Former Secretary of State Madeleine Albright has gone as far to say, "just remember there's a special place in hell for women who don't help each other,"[10] implying women who did not vote for Hillary Clinton are deserving of eternal damnation.

The #MeToo Movement

The #MeToo movement of women stepping forward and publicly sharing experiences of sexual harassment has brought many morally corrupt men to their rightful place of public shame. However, it has also put many good, honorable, respectful men on high alert and changed behaviors in the workplace that have the potential to set women back in their careers - not out of malice, but to avoid the perception of impropriety.

Men who are in positions of authority must now be acutely aware of the social lens through which their lives are being viewed. Because it only takes one person to make an accusation, many men, including Mike Pence, are now re-instituting the so-called "Billy Graham Rule" and are hesitant to be alone with any woman other than their spouse.

This trend recently came to a head in the media when Robert Foster, a Mississippi gubernatorial candidate, declined to be shadowed for a day by a female journalist to "avoid any decision that may evoke suspicion or compromise our marriage."[11]

Foster was subsequently lambasted in the *Washington Post,* which claimed that his refusal was demeaning to all women. The piece argued that either his marriage must lack the trust necessary for a successful relationship, or that he must believe women can't be trusted - or he can't be trusted around them.

Isn't there another option missing? One that has nothing to do with trust or the quality of his marriage, and everything to do with simply avoiding situations that could lead to false accusations of inappropriate actions or comments?

Can you blame a public figure for playing it safe? We all want to believe the best in each other and in mankind, but people do lie - often.

Even worse, the lie doesn't even have to originate from one of the two people in the room. Anyone can make an accusation that something inappropriate happened between two other people, and once that seed is planted, it's nearly impossible to keep it from growing.

To see a real-life example of this, look no further than the 2016 presidential campaign of Senator Ted Cruz. The *National Enquirer* accused the Texas Senator of having an affair with five different women, despite not having a single shred of proof. This led the hashtag #CruzSexScandal to trend worldwide on Twitter, creating a media frenzy and putting doubts in the minds of voters as to whether or not Cruz had integrity.

This fiasco didn't just impact the Cruz campaign. What do you think happened to those women? Their careers and reputations were irrevocably damaged. That damage will live on in perpetuity through the pervasive permanence of the Internet, where a quick Google search by a potential future employer will yield results of involvement in a scandal. Talk about a step backward for female empowerment.

It is truly a damned-if-you-do, damned-if-you-don't situation, but it is hard to blame a public figure from taking precautions to make sure his reputation is protected from baseless claims of others. Unfortunately for women wishing to be involved in politics, this leads to a situation where political leaders refuse to be alone with women.

We have gotten to a stage of the #MeToo movement where many companies have literally considered banning handshakes at work. Yes, handshakes! Handshakes, while a delicate art in and of themselves, have always been considered a professional and even necessary greeting in a business environment. Yet, a recent survey by Total Jobs found that three out of four people want all physical contact banned at work. After all, this would remove confusion over what kind of touching is appropriate.[12]

In the same vein, never being alone with a woman other than your wife removes all confusion about what kind of interaction is appropriate.

The left is right about one thing: *"The most harmful aspect of the Graham rule is this: It keeps women out of the room. It says that men can forward their careers via mentoring sessions, golf games and brainstorming lunches, but women cannot. . . The rule prevents women from climbing to the top of their careers because the men who have the power to help them get there won't even let them in the room."*[13]

> The Left claims to be advocates of feminism, yet in a few short years has created an environment that has made upward mobility more difficult for women.

Yet, the situation they are faced with has left many men with no other choice but to abide by it. The Left claims to be advocates of feminism, yet in a few short years has created an environment that has made upward mobility more difficult for women.

This manufactured culture war is getting out of hand. We live in a world where a liberal man who decides to identify as a woman is a feminist, but a conservative woman who believes the life of her unborn daughter should be protected is not. A world where a man can be thrown out of society based on an accusation without due process but is criticized when he attempts to remove himself from any appearances of impropriety.

This is not how America is supposed to operate. Men should not be afraid to hire and work in collaboration with women in the workplace without being accused of being a scoundrel. A woman should be able to consider herself a feminist and advocate for the betterment of her gender without having to support positions contrary to her personal or religious beliefs.

How are we ever going to solve the world's major problems if we are unwilling to even get in a room and have conversations with one another? Ellen DeGeneres and former President George W. Bush experienced this firsthand when they happened to sit next to each other during a football game. The outrage surrounding their ability to be civil to each other and (gasp!) generally enjoy each other's company even though they had disagreements on policy was out of control. Shutting down discussion, even on a position with which you vehemently disagree, is short-sighted and dangerous for our democracy. Yet, it is more prevalent every day.

Regardless of our ideological beliefs, we share this country, and whether we like to admit it or not, we share a lot of the same values and goals for our lives. So why are we so unwilling to talk to others who hold different beliefs from us?

Tribalism

For the first time in history, we have the ability to filter ourselves into echo chambers of like-minded opinions through social media. No longer are issues discussed face-to-face in the public square, but instead keyboard warriors receive constant affirmation from like-minded individuals that, not only is their perspective correct, but all other perspectives are irrelevant.

In other words, tribalism has taken root in our country. Former Secretary of Defense Jim Mattis lamented this in an editorial in the Wall Street Journal.

> *Unlike in the past, where we were unified and drew in allies, currently our own commons seems to be breaking apart. . . We are dividing into hostile tribes cheering against each other, fueled by emotion and a mutual disdain that jeopardizes our future, instead of rediscovering our common ground and finding solutions.*
>
> *All Americans need to recognize that our democracy is an experiment—and one that can be reversed. We all know that we're better than our current politics. Tribalism must not be allowed to destroy our experiment.*[14]

Even former President Barack Obama has noticed this: *"This idea of purity and you're never compromised and you're always politically 'woke' and all that stuff. You should get over that quickly. The world is messy, there are ambiguities. People who do really good stuff have flaws. People who you are fighting may love their kids. And share certain things with you."*[15]

In his piece titled, "Against Identity Politics," Francis Fukuyama discusses how he believes the shift toward identity politics took root:

"Democratic societies are fracturing into segments based on ever-narrower identities, threatening the possibility of deliberation and collective action by society as a whole. This is a road that leads only to state breakdown and, ultimately, failure."[16]

No wonder we feel like we are constantly walking on eggshells when discussing political issues in the public square. Sadly, absolute truth has become a thing of the past, as each identity group on both the Left and the Right declares the other's perspective as "fake news."

For decades, we have allowed women on the Left to carry the banner for our cause, and as a result, we have been left out of the dialogue. We cannot allow this to continue any longer.

I sat down with Congresswoman Cathy McMorris Rodgers, a trailblazer by all accounts, to talk more about women in politics. Elected in 2004, she is one of the highest-ranking Republican women in Congress and served as chair of the House Republican Caucus from 2013-19. Prior to her time in Congress, McMorris Rodgers served in the Washington House of Representatives, where she was elected Minority Leader in 2001, becoming the first woman to lead a caucus in state history. She was the 200th woman elected to Congress out of the roughly 11,000 individuals who have served, and the only woman in history to give birth three times while serving.

When I asked her something every woman could do today to make a difference, she had great insight:

> *I would encourage each of us to give thought to just one thing we can be doing. We put so much pressure on ourselves that somehow, we are going to solve it all, and that's not going to happen. Think about one thing.*
>
> *We need people to think about what they can be doing to be contributors and not just be looking at others to do it. Be a part of the five percent of any organization that actually steps up and get things done.*
>
> *There is a lot of conversation right now about isolationism, that we are all so busy and that we aren't prioritizing relationships. Be a force for positivity and be an encourager of others. I am wary about how much of politics is about tearing one another down and how that has just dripped into our society. We have a lot of critics who are quick to point out when someone is doing something wrong - let's be an encourager and start building each other up again.*
>
> *I find myself thinking back to JFK when he said: 'Ask not what your country can do for you – ask what you can do for your country.' We need a revival where each one of us is asking that question, and it starts in our families and communities.*

All of us are capable of finding one thing we can do to contribute and make our communities and nation a better place. Simply caring and showing up is half the battle.

The Left understands this, which is why it has been so successful in controlling the narrative in recent years. They know that "the squeaky wheel gets the grease" and that the war is not won in a single night, but through a series of small victories and incremental change.

> All of us are capable of finding one thing we can do to contribute and make our communities and nation a better place. Simply caring and showing up is half the battle.

Because these activists care, they are more prone to show up to town hall forums, create advocacy groups, call their lawmakers, sign petitions, and raise money. Simply showing up has allowed them to incrementally achieve their goals in city halls and state legislatures around the country.

There is a sleeping giant out there of women who feel completely unrepresented by our current women's movement. I am here to tell you that you aren't alone. Millions of women just like you across this country are frustrated and disappointed. It's time to channel that energy into action.

KEY INSIGHTS

- The Left has overtaken the "women's movement," claiming to speak for all women and working to silence alternative viewpoints.
- By limiting "women's issues" to reproductive care, women's voices on other critical issues, such as tax policy, are diminished.
- The #MeToo movement did a lot of good, but has also left unintended consequences in its wake, creating new barriers for women to get ahead.
- Tribalism is pushing us further into separate corners, making it more difficult to find common ground and ultimately endangering our democracy.
- The squeaky wheel gets the grease. Caring enough to simply show up is half the battle.

CALL TO ACTION

Channel frustration and disappointment into action. What is the one thing you can do to make a difference? Be part of the small percentage of people who actually show up to the council meeting, call your representative, or donate to a candidate.

3

Being a Conservative Woman in Modern America (You Are Not Alone!)

The direction our country has drifted when it comes to freedom of speech and respectful discourse is scary.

It wasn't that long ago that parents were deemed successful if their children graduated high school with a strong moral compass and a sense of values. Now morality no longer correlates with Judeo-Christian beliefs, but instead is evaluated based upon how dedicated you are to the altar of so-called "tolerance" and social justice.

Our country has been polarized between Republicans and Democrats, liberals and conservatives for decades, but now differences in ideology have led to a shift in our culture and hostility toward those who push back on the latest leftist agenda.

The Leftist Agenda

Political battles that are played out in the mainstream media every day are often won, not by logic and facts, but by emotions.

Social justice warriors are not utilizing reason in their crusade to move us closer and closer to socialism. They are counting on you to side with them by tugging on your heartstrings. To the casual observer, their pursuit of a utopian society where everyone is equal seems compassionate, even if in reality history has proven time and time again that socialism only delivers poverty, misery, and ruin.

Militant environmentalists claim that the world will end in twelve years due to climate change. We all want to be good stewards of our environment, and we have made huge progress in doing so. Since 1970 the six major pollutants in America monitored by the EPA have plunged by 73 percent, while the U.S. economy grew 262 percent and its population by 60 percent.[17] The United States is finally energy-independent, with affordable and reliable energy helping to drive the economy and provide a high quality of life for Americans.

Despite these facts, the Left is pushing the Green New Deal, which would financially devastate families. The American Action Forum estimates that, between 2020 and 2029, the energy and environmental components of the Green New Deal would cost $8.3 trillion to $12.3 trillion, or $52,000 to $72,000 per household. The total Green New Deal program, including the jobs and "social justice" policies, would cost $51.1 trillion to $92.9 trillion, or $316,010 to $419,010 per household.[18]

Meanwhile, lack of access to reliable, affordable energy is keeping women all over the world in poverty. Arduous tasks that require hard labor, like cooking, gathering water, and caring for children is almost solely the responsibility of wives, mothers, and daughters in places without electricity. The Texas Public Policy Foundation lays out the case clearly:

> *According to UNICEF, women and girls around the world spend 200 million hours a day walking to collect water. This is time-consuming and physically taxing work, requiring women to walk more than three miles on average carrying immensely heavy loads while also putting themselves at risk for physical and sexual assault . . . That burden could be lifted with access to electricity to pump the water where it is needed.*

To make matters worse, three billion people worldwide lack access to safe cooking and heating fuels and are instead forced to burn wood, animal dung, kerosene, or coal. Girls in these households spend more than an hour every day collecting fuel, only to put themselves in more danger when they return home. Sadly, 3.8 million people die prematurely every year as a result of toxic pollutants released when these fuels are burned in close quarters. Naturally, most are women and girls.

If every community around the globe had the same affordable, reliable, and abundant energy as we enjoy in the United States, the untapped potential of millions of women in developing nations would be unleashed. . . Energy offers more than light and warmth to women in need. It offers freedom.[19]

This is not a convenient narrative for leftist activists and politicians who are using talking points decrying fossil fuels to motivate their base and raise money for campaigns and causes. But, having facts on your side is no longer relevant in our political arena.

Look no further than Greta Thunberg's speech before the United Nations Climate Action Summit. Thunberg captured the media's attention worldwide - a young activist arguing passionately for a cause she believes in. But her speech was short on facts and long on emotional hyperbole. She exclaimed, *"You have stolen my dreams and my childhood with your empty words . . . People are suffering. People are dying. Entire ecosystems are collapsing. We are in the beginning of a mass extinction."*[20]

If only she could channel that passion into advocating for the millions of women in the world whose lives would be immeasurably improved, and even saved, by access to electricity of any kind.

Another example of political theater is being played out in the uproar against Chick-fil-A.

This chain is notorious for having friendly staff and the best customer service (not to mention, the most delicious chicken sandwiches and lemonade). The corporation and individual franchisees are also frequently active in local communities and a variety of nonprofits that seek to make the world a better place.

Yet, the City of San Antonio recently voted against allowing Chick-fil-A in its airport, citing contributions to the Salvation Army as being bigoted against the LGBT community. The Salvation Army is a faith-based non-profit that serves more than 58.4 million meals and provides 10.8 million nights of shelter per year to those in need in the United States. With proceeds from thrift shops, they also fund the largest free residential drug and alcohol rehabilitation program in the country.[21]

We are past the point of legitimate outrage based on actual discrimination. You are now considered a bigot if you express an opinion that clashes with popular culture. At least in the case of Chick-fil-A, there have been some positive outcomes, both in terms of profits as well as religious liberty.

Chick-fil-A is now the third largest restaurant chain in the United States, and its sales have tripled in just the last ten years.[22] Additionally, due to the recent actions in San Antonio, state officials passed legislation prohibiting governmental entities from punishing businesses or people for contributions to religious organizations.[23]

By providing a high-quality product and great service at an affordable price, Chick-fil-A was able to weather a media onslaught and not only survive but grow. The company's actions also helped usher in new legislation that protects the religious rights of all business owners.

While stories like this are encouraging, I am afraid we will see fewer successes if we cannot turn the tide on the censorship, de-platforming, and de-monetization of conservative viewpoints on social media.

Every day, monopolistic social media platforms such as Facebook, Twitter, and Instagram are silencing and discouraging dialogue on societal challenges that are far from settled. This "my way or the highway" attitude on opinions is forcing mass approval on fringe issues that would have never reached prominence in a pre-Internet era.

No longer are you simply attacked if you express controversial viewpoints online. Now you are censored, your post is deleted, and you can get suspended or banned if you offend enough people. And, depending on where you work, you may get fired.

Is it just me, or is it getting a little crazy around here?

Ten years ago, would you have ever thought we would be debating allowing men in women's bathrooms? Much less, could you have fathomed social media companies would silence and censor a parent for expressing anger at their daughter being taught in public school that she may, in fact, be a boy?

We are bending biological sex in a way that is beyond comprehension. Because of America's history of discrimination against various marginalized groups, society has allowed the pendulum to swing so far in the other direction that you are no longer allowed to disagree or even question any aspect of the transgender movement.

As Comedian Dave Chappelle points out in his latest stand-up, *Sticks and Stones*: "*The rule is that no matter what you do in your artistic expression, you are never, ever, allowed to upset the alphabet people (the LGBT community). Say LeBron James, uh, changed his gender. You know what I mean? Okay. Can he stay in the NBA, or, because he's a woman, does he have to go to the WNBA where he will score 840 points a game?*"

While Chappelle's question seems like just another punch-line, it is based in reality when it comes to professional sports. Athletic competitions are frequently allowing biological men who identify as transgender women to compete in women's sporting events. In 2018, a biological male won a women's cycling world championship. That same year, a man who identifies as a woman won an NCAA women's track championship.[24]

Jennifer Wagner-Assali, a cyclist who won a bronze medal behind a transgender man said of the situation, *"I do feel that hard-fought freedoms for women's sport are being eroded. If we continue to let this happen, there will be men's sports and co-ed sports, but there won't be any women's sports."*[25]

> "I do feel that hard-fought freedoms for women's sport are being eroded. If we continue to let this happen, there will be men's sports and co-ed sports, but there won't be any women's sports."

Have you heard about Drag Queen Story Time at your local library? It is a movement in cities all across the country. Many public libraries spend tax dollars to host regular story times where drag queens read to children. When this issue was before the city council in Austin following the end of my term, all 11 members voted to support it. More than that, the people who came to the meeting to speak about their concerns were labeled as hateful, demeaned, and even spat on.

A former drag queen who actually opposed the idea pleaded with the Council to think about who this initiative was really serving: the children, or some political cause. He was told from the dais to "sashay away" (how's that for tolerance?).[26] And the organization he was a part of was labeled as a "hate group" by the Southern Poverty Law Center because of its stance on issues like this.

Moreover, school districts across the country are adopting a curriculum that teaches students as young as fifth grade that gender is a "spectrum" and that you can be a boy, a girl, or anything in between. Is this really what's in the best interest of children, or is the Left pushing an adult narrative to make themselves feel good?

While you must now be 21 years old to buy a pack of cigarettes in the Lone Star State, Austin Independent School District will teach children as young as elementary school lessons on sexual orientation, gender identity, and sexually transmitted diseases.[27]

The newly adopted curriculum instructs children as young as 3rd grade to avoid using the words "mother" and "father" to describe their parents, arguing that this can "limit their understanding of gender." Instead, students are urged to use words like "parent" and "guardian."

In another lesson, students are asked to define words like "pansexual" in a matching game. They learn that a traditional doctor "decides" what sex someone is at birth.

The curriculum adopted for students in 3rd through 8th grade also recommends resources that describe sexual behavior in detail and includes information about how to get birth control pills and an abortion without telling their parents.[28]

This is not mainstream America. This is not what mothers (or fathers!) expect their children to be taught in the classroom.

While children should be learning that everyone is deserving of love and respect regardless of their circumstances, these lessons are instead politicizing sex in a way that normalizes risky fringe behavior.

One frustrated parent, Matt Pennies, attended the Austin school board meeting approving the new curriculum, and said: *"I get the sensitivities around the LGBT issues. I tried to say this, but I was drowned out by the chaos — even in a strictly heterosexual context, this content is just so aggressive. It's just so much, so soon."*[29]

For Matt and many other parents like him, it is becoming more and more difficult to express any view that doesn't fit into the "progressive" narrative, which is continually being pushed further and further left. Those who do can now be silenced in the public square.

> It is becoming more and more difficult to express any view that doesn't fit into the "progressive" narrative, which is continually being pushed further and further left.
> Those who do can now be silenced in the public square.

Despite the outcry from many parents, the new curriculum in Austin was passed unanimously. And, don't think this is just happening in Austin. School districts across Texas and the nation are quickly moving in this direction.

Meanwhile, the United States ranks 24th in both reading and science and 71st in math, according to one of the biggest cross-national tests that measures key skills among 15-year-olds in developed and developing countries.[30] We are failing to teach our students basic skills while continually being distracted by the latest social justice causes.

Sadly, these are just a few examples of the culture war we are fighting in our country today. The challenge of defending your beliefs publicly is daunting, but we cannot allow ourselves to be bullied into silence.

How are we supposed to survive, much less raise kids, in an increasingly hostile environment toward any viewpoint that does not reflect the agenda of the extreme Left? How are we supposed to change public sentiment if we are silenced every time we express a thought that is controversial or not politically correct from a leftist perspective?

Like the frustrated parent quoted above, who was representing a common point of view but was drowned out by a sea of activists, you sometimes find yourself in a setting where your viewpoint is the minority opinion. It may be at work, a social setting, or even a family gathering. Remember that however "against the odds" you may feel at that moment, millions of others share your outlook - you are not alone. Advocating from a minority viewpoint in such a setting can be difficult but standing up for what you believe is more important.

Here are some tips to make sure you are as effective as possible in your arguments:

- Always be respectful, even if you're not shown the same respect in return.
- Base your arguments in facts. This gives you confidence and keeps disagreements from becoming personal.
- Choose your forum wisely. Don't expect to change someone's mind with a Facebook post. Think about whether the environment will be conducive to a productive discussion.
- Endeavor not to be offended. Political discussions can get heated, but not taking things personally will help you keep a level head and get your point across in the most constructive way.
- Don't respond to false premises. Leading questions are designed to put you on the defensive. Instead, circle back to reiterate your key points.
- Write your key points down for reference, if needed, to help you stay focused on what you want to address.
- Don't back down. Fiercely defend your point of view. Even if you feel overwhelmed, intimidated, or outnumbered, know you're not alone!

You Are Not Alone

Modern feminism in the current political climate has left conservative women feeling lost, alone, and completely misunderstood. When not being overrun by a "women's march" that doesn't represent their values, they're having hushed conversations with friends over dinner, careful not to be overheard by the judgmental ears of nearby diners. They're overwhelmed by self-righteous rhetoric on social media. They're scared to speak up at work for fear of belittlement and exclusion. And they're left wondering, "Am I the only one who feels this way?" It's discouraging, deflating, and demoralizing.

But, they're not alone.

I cannot tell you how many conversations I have had with women who are afraid to speak up and feel isolated in their beliefs about politics and the world around them.

For years, liberal "feminists" have used fearmongering and public shaming to silence alternative voices and make moderate and conservative women feel like gender traitors to the cause of advancing women's rights.

One tactic that has been used again and again is the use of misleading statistics to convince women that they are the victims of systematic societal discrimination. Perhaps the most famous example is the issue of the so-called gender pay gap.

Leftist icons from Hillary Clinton to Elizabeth Warren travel the country telling women they are making almost a quarter less than men, and therefore advocate for government intervention.

What they don't tell you is that the 77 cents for every dollar statistic that they parrot looks only at the median earnings and doesn't take into account factors such as experience, education, occupation or even the number of hours worked. As a result, the American Association of University Women (AAUW), a feminist organization founded in 1881, found that the gap shrinks to just 6.6 cents when you factor in the *choices* people make when choosing their occupation.[31] While progress is still to be made, the truth is much less angering than the misleading statistic.

Some occupations pay more than others, which is inevitable, but those occupations also likely require more skills, education, or time. This has nothing to do with gender, but with the qualifications and requirements of a job and the personal choices made by both women and men.

Let's take for example the occupations of teaching and engineering. Women make up 77 percent of all teachers in the United States,[32] while they make up only 13 percent of engineers.[33] Engineers on average earn $87,370 a year, while teachers earn $62,150.[34] While we can do more to ensure that women are equally encouraged to pursue high paying professions, we can assume that the women who went into teaching generally preferred that career over being an engineer, and vice versa.

How could this income "inequality" be resolved by the government? Do we force an equal number of men and women to pursue every profession, against their will? Of course not! Should we require every occupation be made up of an equal number of women and men, regardless of whether or not have any interest in their forced field of work? Of course not!

Some women prefer to work part-time, some women do not want to climb the corporate ladder, and clearly some women prefer to be teachers instead of engineers. Women don't want to be forced into a profession in which they do not want to be. Women tend to value work-life balance and the ability to negotiate flex time. Some women would prefer to ask to work from home a few days a week rather than ask for a raise.

These are all choices they should be free to make. A government-mandated, one-size-fits-all pay scale takes this flexibility away from women.

Women (and men for that matter) want to have more money available to provide for their families and improve their quality of life. But ginning up a false narrative about a gender pay gap that actually takes freedoms and choices away from women is not the way to do it.

My notion of "having it all" may look a lot different from yours. You might have no interest in having children and instead want to build a successful career before traveling the world. You may have decided that being a stay-at-home mom to your kids is what makes you most happy. Or, you may have landed somewhere in the middle, like me.

All of these options are okay, and no one should be able to decide the life you want to live, except for you. Isn't that what feminism should be all about - having the ability to choose the type of life we want for ourselves? It is a luxury that many women did not have in previous decades and fought hard to ensure for future generations.

Can't we all celebrate and support each other for our own unique decisions?

Instead of being distracted by false narratives on financial matters, our time and energy is best spent advocating for issues that most significantly impact our household income, such as tax reform. The amount of money we lose to taxes is much more than the 6.6 cents that we lose to a wage gap, and we should spend more of our time fighting to keep more of what we have earned.

> Instead of being distracted by false narratives on financial matters, our time and energy is best spent advocating for issues that most significantly impact our household income, such as tax reform. The amount of money we lose to taxes is much more than the 6.6 cents that we lose to a wage gap, and we should spend more of our time fighting to keep more of what we have earned.

An Important Voice

While on the Austin City Council, I became notorious as a fiscal hawk fighting to lower the tax burden on my constituents. Every year when we crafted the city's budget, which was in excess of $4 billion, my staff and I worked to see not where we should spend the money, but where it was being wasted.

I tried to practice what I preached, saving money from my personal office budget every year to give back to my district in the form of improvements to our local parks. I had the budget for four staff members but found that I could get the job done with three full time and one part time employee instead. Our office was allocated funds for expenses such as travel to conferences and food that I chose not to use. I squirreled away the savings every month so that I had a small pot of money at the end of the year. With the funds I had saved, I was able to replace old exercise equipment at a local park, provide shade over playscapes, and renovate trailheads. These were small but valuable projects to my constituents. And, it was important to me to demonstrate that reductions could be made if you treated every dollar like it was your own.

But when it comes to the city's budget, once a government program is started, it's nearly impossible to get rid of it. In fact, it's nearly impossible just to keep the program's funding from automatically growing year over year. There were plenty of times that waste and abuse were identified by our city auditor, but there was not always action taken by the council to do something about it.

Early on in my service, I noticed continual issues with customers being overcharged by Austin's water utility. As an example, an elderly woman with no pool, sprinkler system, or leaks received an $800 water bill one month, well out of line with the $75 bill she usually paid. She was on a fixed income and absolutely beside herself with worry. She was working to come up with a payment plan that would keep her captive for the next 12 months to pay off the bill. When I received similar calls, I pushed for a series of audits that uncovered consistent errors being made, and ultimately was able to institute a safety net program for people who received a bill with an unusual and unexplained spike. Unfortunately, this process was long and difficult, taking several years to implement.

Many other problems went unaddressed by a council that was resistant to change and protected unionized city employees at all costs. When we found out that oil changes and basic maintenance for our city's fleet of thousands of vehicles cost two to three times as much as what it would if those services were provided by the private sector, they turned a blind eye.[35] The Council was unwilling to outsource the work despite the fact that constituents' hard-earned money was being wasted.

There was one program that allowed anyone who emailed the city to say that they were starting a business or buying a house to receive a handout of up to $3,500. Under the auspices of a matched savings account program, the city would match the funds supposedly going to one of these uses by a ratio of 8:1. If you had $500, the city would provide you with a blank check for an additional $3,500. There was no due diligence done to qualify the recipient or find out what the money ultimately went toward. There was no accountability for the program.[36] Even this information didn't trigger an immediate halt to the program.

Another time, I examined information provided to the Council regarding the workforce development contracts the city had in place. These contracts provided money to outside organizations that administered programs to assist those in need with education and job training skills in order to help them find employment or move into a higher paying job. The results were clear - the city had no coordinated plan for implementing these programs and was not collecting the data necessary in order to evaluate the success. We did not know if participants actually got a job or received the wage increase that was being targeted after completing the programs.

It was shocking to uncover that the city was spending $41,000 per participant in one program, meaning that we could have paid for tuition at the local community college for each participant for much less than taxpayers spent on the workforce training.[37] With contracts totaling $6 million per year, a lot of money was at stake. Even worse, the people who needed the services were not being provided what they were promised. Yet, despite my best efforts, and to my continued bewilderment, the contracts remain funded. The contracts were defended regardless of their failure to perform, and no reductions were made.

My voice on the Council consistently helped to bring attention to the wasteful spending that was going on in our city. While reform did not always happen at all, or as quickly as it should have, the increased media attention helped residents to better understand the decisions their council members were making and helped me build support for transparency and accountability initiatives.

There were also times that fiscal responsibility and common sense prevailed. During my first budget cycle, I was able to do something unprecedented - actually give money back to the taxpayers. As the Council crafted the budget, my staff and I worked to find $4 million of savings. This money was not attached to a particular program and would not require a cut to any project. It was sitting in an account, unused. We were thrilled to have come upon a significant sum that could be returned to the people who owned it without ruffling the feathers of a specific department or pet project. We drafted an amendment and proposed it hopefully. It passed! I was elated, but my excitement didn't last long.

The Council wasn't done. Eyeing the large pot of money that was now unallocated, council members began spending it. Over the course of the next few minutes, I lost a series of quick votes, where $3 million of the $4 million that I had just saved was spent, newly dedicated to a variety of different causes. There was only $1 million left, and I pleaded with my colleagues not to spend it. This was money that had been taken from the taxpayers for no reason, and they deserved it back. Despite protestations from some of my big-spending colleagues, I won a narrow vote to give it back to the people who had earned it by applying the money to lower the property tax rate.

While it wasn't as much as I wanted, it was something, and that counted. It was the first time ever in the City of Austin that this had been done. Every year during my tenure, I fought for similar measures.

It was years earlier that I developed my passion for accountability and property tax reform. I had been a Realtor only a couple of months when my eyes were opened to what a huge problem property taxes had truly become for the City of Austin.

I had a young, middle-class client named Sarah who had worked hard for years getting her finances to a place where she could finally afford to buy a house.

Instead of spending all of her monthly paycheck on expensive dinners and vacations, she had diligently set aside everything she could each month to afford a down payment on a house.

We spent weeks, even months, searching for the perfect house within her modest budget before we found something she fell in love with. She was approved for the loan, and it looked like she was finally going to accomplish her dream of owning a home.

Before we were set to put in an offer, Sarah decided to do the math one more time and estimate what her property taxes would be each month for the next few years. What she discovered was that although she could afford the taxes this year, the city was annually raising property taxes at such a rate that it was unlikely her salary would grow enough to cover the difference within a few years.

With property taxes on track to double every nine years, increases in electric and water rates and other city fees, she would need a salary hike of at least 8% per year to keep up. She certainly couldn't expect an 8% increase in her salary every single year for the foreseeable future.

Sarah decided not to purchase the home after all, not because she couldn't afford it now, but because she feared she wouldn't be able to afford to pay the property taxes in future years.

I wish I could tell you this story was unique, but it happens every day. And worse, many families buy houses unaware of how their tax burden will accelerate in the future, and end up losing their homes, forced to uproot their families and their lives.

Property taxes - or some other form of tax depending on which state you live in - aren't as sexy as the gender pay gap, but they sure have just as big of an impact on the cost of living and our ability to improve the quality of life for our families.

Tackling Fear

My fear of public speaking crept up on me in college, ironically, when I took a public speaking class. A class designed to give me more confidence and practice getting up in front of people, instead served to incite pangs of anxiety. When it came time to deliver our most recent assignment in class, I never volunteered to go first. But, the longer I waited and the more presentations from my fellow students I sat through, the higher my heart rate increased. Eventually, all of the other students had given their pitches and there was no one left to hide behind. By the time it was my turn, I was warm and blotchy, and my voice was shaky. The funny thing about anxiety is that it's a self-fulfilling cycle. The more often you're anxious about a certain thing, the more your body learns that this is how it is supposed to react when you're in that situation. That means the more times I had to get up in front of the class to speak, the more consistent my anxiety became.

Even still, I made it out of the class with a passable grade. After graduation, I was mostly successful in avoiding public speaking in my adult life. Despite having a degree in international business from one of the top ranked schools in the country, being an event planner sounded much more fun than a corporate nine to five. Making almost no money and without much of a plan for the future, my parents were not thrilled with this decision. Luckily for them, it only took six months of dealing with brides looking for someone to blame for the rain on their wedding day, their mother-in-law's dress choice, or a rogue bridesmaid for me to realize that this was not how I wanted to spend my time.

From there, I needed a change of scenery and headed to San Antonio to work for a wine distributor. I met the delivery trucks at six o'clock in the morning, six days a week, and stocked the shelves at nine H-E-B grocery stores. Working on commission, I had to convince the grocery manager at each store that the wine brands I was offering would be a popular seller that week. Representing certain brands, it was a highly competitive environment, working against other salespeople with similar pitches about why the manager should buy wine to fill their shelves from them. (Next time you see a big wine display at your local grocery store, know that it is because the wine salesperson needed to sell a certain number of cases to meet their target for that month and the store got a good deal, not because the wine is particularly good.) There was a lot of manual labor involved - hauling a pallet of wine boxes off of a truck, getting the wine from the back of the store out to the shelves, carrying the individual cases from the pallet to the right spot on the floor, filling the holes by restocking the bottles that had sold the day before, condensing the size of the pallet by combining the half-empty cases, and pulling the pallet back to its designated place of storage. Then, doing it all over again at eight other stores that same day, and repeating the process over again the next.

But there was no public speaking.

Needless to say, I was one of the only women in this male-dominated, labor-intensive, highly competitive job. And in the year that I spent doing it, I learned how to navigate this environment with skills that ultimately served me well in politics. I had to hold my own, watch my back, and develop good working relationships with others I worked with, even when we were working against each other.

Once I realized that my heart still remained in Austin, with Caleb, and with policy work, I moved back and parlayed my previous internship at the State Capitol into a Legislative Aide position. In this role, I made sure that the elected officials I worked for were prepared for their speaking engagements by researching issues and writing talking points, but I was rarely required to stand up in front of a crowd. By watching others do it, I picked up some tips about how to effectively speak to the media (don't be distracted by leading questions - always bring the conversation back to the message you want to convey) and handle a controversial issue (respectfully but firmly reiterate your position).

Once I became a Chief of Staff, there were times that I needed to speak on behalf of my boss, usually at meetings or events they weren't able to attend due to scheduling. While I should say this gave me good practice, I still avoided these situations at all costs.

But when it came to running for office, my frustration at the city and my desire to change the direction ultimately outweighed my fear of public speaking. At first, I tried not to think about it, and downplayed to myself and to others the amount of public speaking that would be required. How many "debates" would there really be for a city council seat? (There were a lot.) Even if I was elected, how often would I really have to speak in large crowds? (Every week, from the dais, with a microphone, in the

Council chambers full of media, city staff, and Austin residents.) Surely the media will want to talk to other people, not me? (As the only conservative, they always called me to hear the "other" side of the story.)

My first real test was my campaign kickoff. You know those memes where people try to decorate baked goods or recreate a project that they saw on Pinterest, and the finished product is a total disaster that looks nothing like the "inspiration" photo? It was kind of like that. I definitely did not nail it. Several hundred people were in attendance. I wrote my entire speech on notecards that I bent back and forth nervously in my sweaty hands. When it was time, I read from the cards, looking up at the attendees as often as I was able, and I got through it. It wasn't particularly inspiring, moving, or passionate, but it got my point across. Taxes were too damn high, and I wanted to do something about it.

On the campaign trail, I knew I had to talk to as many voters as possible, including groups who wanted to hear from the candidates. I started in environments where I felt most comfortable: the local Republican clubs and women's organizations. I knew some of the people involved from my work at the Capitol, and they would at least hear me out.

At one of these early speaking engagements, I fumbled through my stump speech and mishandled a couple of questions from the audience that I was not prepared to answer. I felt out of my element, questioning if I was going to be able to get through this campaign after all. Had I made a mistake putting my name on the ballot?

But afterward, three women approached me to ask how they could help me with my campaign. They agreed with what I had to say, even if I didn't say it as eloquently as I would have liked, and they could see that I was in it for the right reasons. I wasn't polished or seasoned, but I was authentic and passionate. In fact, had I been a polished and seasoned politician, my message likely would not have resonated with them like it did.

I wasn't polished or seasoned, but I was authentic and passionate. In fact, had I been a polished and seasoned politician, my message likely would not have resonated with voters and volunteers like it did. In this way, my perceived weakness in public speaking turned into one of my greatest strengths. By allowing my authenticity shine through, it allowed voters, supporters, and volunteers to connect with me in a unique way.

Dede, Judy, and Mary ended up being my secret weapons. They were dedicated block walkers who help to spread the word about my campaign to thousands of voters. They knocked on doors during the work week and nearly every weekend. Rain or shine, I could count on them. More than that, they believed in me and their confidence in me helped me to build confidence in myself. I didn't want to let them down! I would not have won my election without these three amazing women.

In this way, my perceived weakness in public speaking turned into one of my greatest strengths. By allowing my authenticity shine through, it allowed voters, supporters, and volunteers to connect with me in a unique way. I was one of them! People like to vote for candidates who are like them, someone who they would hang out with. It's nice if that candidate is also competent and capable, but approachability goes a long way.

Despite many years of additional practice under my belt, I'm still not polished or articulate. I still get nervous and stumble over my words. And, you can still tell when I'm anxious.

On the city council dais, there were many days that a controversial issue was being discussed, and I knew I had to speak up and voice yet another unpopular opinion in advance of yet another vote that I would lose ten to one. The council chambers would be full of activists from a socialist group pushing their latest policy or members of an organization that received money from the city and wanted more. They clapped when the other council members expressed support for their cause. I fumbled with my microphone and jotted down notes while I waited (and waited) for the Mayor to recognize me to speak. I tried not to look at the news cameras in the back of the room that would be recording my response. I could feel red blotches appear on my neck. There was no way to hide it, despite my best efforts.

But I always spoke up. And, you know what I never had a single supporter say, "I wish you hadn't said that. I wish you had stayed quiet." Quite the opposite. The feedback I would receive later would instead say, "Thank you for standing up for us. Thank you for speaking out."

Putting myself in a position where I had no choice but to face my own personal fear not only helped me grow as a person, but was also a small sacrifice in comparison to the immense gratitude that I received for representing people who had no one else standing up for them.

Public speaking is a reality of life every day for me now. I have a regular spot on Austin's talk radio station, and I'm constantly recording episodes of my podcast, also titled Step Up. Reporters for TV media, which I came to learn was an incredibly effective and painless way to get my message out, still call me for interviews when they want to hear the other side of the story.

It would have been a shame to allow my small fear get in the way.

Reflecting on how there is likely never a perfect time for you or your family to run for office, Congresswoman McMorris Rodgers said this:

> I am a working mom and there are millions of working moms in America. It is tough.
>
> I was 35 and single when I was elected to Congress and I have wondered at different times if anyone would have been

able to convince me to run for Congress after I had three kids. And I don't know the answer to that question . . .

There are times that it is hard, but I think that any working mom struggles with that and struggles being gone when you want to be home. And then when you are home you are thinking about some of the demands of the job. So, some days go better than others, but I have found a lot of fulfillment in what I am doing. I also believe that it is an important perspective that I bring as a working mom, considering that so many working moms are doing this in a whole list of other jobs in America. We need to celebrate and encourage moms and the roles they play in our lives.

I get it. We're busy, overwhelmed, and exhausted just taking care of our families and/or managing our careers. We don't need something else on our plate, especially anything that involves putting yourself out there for the general public to critique and analyze. We are so busy running our lives and trying to keep it all together that we don't consider adding another unnecessary, intimidating thing like running for office until something truly pisses us off and we feel the time is right. As a result, significantly fewer women than men run for office.

We have to get beyond this fear.

Patricia Rucker immigrated to the United States from Venezuela. After meeting and marrying her husband, they had five children together, including two with special needs. Their local public schools didn't offer the kind of support and services she thought her children required, and she made the decision to homeschool all five of them. Yet, her full-time job as a mom and a homeschooling teacher, or the fact that she was a non-native English speaker, didn't stop her from stepping up to run for the West Virginia State Senate when she saw a need. She now serves as a State Senator. She reflected:

If you feel that calling to run, don't let fear get in the way. I was terrified, running against someone who was a lawyer. And, here I was, someone who had never done any public speaking. I just thought I could never do a good job. But people can see that you mean what you say, that you really care. And I think that's more important than being a great speaker or being polished.

I have an accent! I'm not even a native English speaker. But folks really truly care more about what you're trying to do for them. And that's what you're looking for. I've been told by others that I'm giving them hope because they know that I'm actually doing what I said I was going to do, and I'm not a politician trying to scratch my own back or scratch the back of my friends. I'm just representing the average person.

Politics can seem overwhelming, and it often feels impossible to make a real impact. Even when you are fortunate enough to end up in a position where you can affect public policy, things move so slowly that it is easy to get discouraged and give up.

We can't give up. The other side isn't giving up. If anything, the other side is becoming more emboldened and willing to impose its viewpoints on anyone who isn't willing to stand up and fight back.

Ensuring my children have the best possible opportunities to succeed in life will always be my top priority. Yes, that means being active in their lives as a mother, but it also means ensuring that the world they will one day inherit will be better than the world we live in today.

For this to be the case, I must be involved politically. And you must too.

We are the sleeping giant with the most untapped potential. What is it going to take for us to wake up?

KEY INSIGHTS

- Political battles are often fought by playing to emotions instead of relying on facts.
- From the New Green Deal, which would be financially devastating to families, to teaching flexible gender identity to 5th graders, the Left's narrative is moving further and further away from family values and mainstream America.
- Those who disagree, no matter how reasonably, are labeled as hateful and censored in an effort to discredit them. Advocating from a minority viewpoint is challenging but can be done effectively.
- Issues such as the gender pay gap are used as political tools, devaluing individual life choices and overshadowing issues that have a bigger impact on our pocketbooks.
- There is no better way to overcome your fears than by forcing yourself to face them. Your perceived weakness may actually be a strength.
- Stepping outside your comfort zone is daunting, but your voice is needed now more than ever.

CALL TO ACTION

Research organizations that are working to further your ideals (check out Chapter 6 for some ideas). Join! Commit to carving out a small part of your time or money to support their work.

4

A Woman's Touch

Everyone is shaped by their upbringing, and I am no different.

As is true with many people, my principles didn't come from a political textbook or some philosopher's rigid doctrine. They came from watching my parents and seeing firsthand the impact one can have with a strong work ethic and compassion for your neighbors and community.

The chances of my parents ever meeting was slim to none.

As a young woman, my grandmother took off to South America in search of adventure. What she found was my grandfather, an American foreman for a gold mine, running operations in the remote jungles of Venezuela.

My mother, Susan, was born a couple years later and spent the first three years of her life living in the dense jungle surrounding the mining operation hundreds of miles from civilization. There were no grocery stores, medical care, or modern amenities, and little-to-no contact with the civilized world.

To keep his sanity, my grandfather would have bundles of newspapers shipped to him each month from the United States. Every Sunday, he would sit on the porch and read a newspaper, even if it was a month old, to stay current on events happening in the world.

Eventually, my mother and her older brother Paul, age seven, were speaking more Spanish than English, and with her school years approaching, my grandparents decided it was time to move back to America.

Sadly, a couple years later my grandfather passed away, leaving my grandmother a widow with two young children in

Phoenix, Arizona, where my mom would spend the rest of her childhood.

My dad, Rex, on the other hand, had a more traditional upbringing. He was born in Massachusetts and grew up in Long Island, New York. He was very athletic and spent his childhood focused on sports.

He attended the University of South Carolina and majored in journalism. He would go on to work for the university as an admissions counselor, where he would assist the university president on projects from time to time.

The president was very involved with an orphanage in Cuernavaca, Mexico called Nuestros Pequeños Hermanos (NPH). Once a year, he would go down to the orphanage for board meetings to discuss potential partnerships with the university.

NPH was run by Father William B. Wasson, a priest who began the orphanage after saving a young boy from a lengthy prison sentence by taking him under his guardianship. The boy had been caught stealing from the church donation box because he was hungry, and Father Wasson took pity on him. The judge agreed to place the boy and eight other troubled youth under Father Wasson's care, and over time an orphanage was born.

Father Wasson was from Phoenix, Arizona and was regularly featured in local newspapers and magazines for his efforts taking care of the children of Cuernavaca. Shortly after my mother graduated from Arizona State University, my grandmother showed her an article about the orphanage that detailed the wonderful work that was being done there.

My mom's heart was moved, and she decided to learn more about the operation and see if they had any opportunities for her to help. Within a week, she had a job offer and was preparing to move to Mexico and help the orphanage with fundraising.

If you have ever watched late-night TV and seen the advertisements for sponsoring children in underdeveloped countries for a dollar a day, that was essentially my mom's job. In her words, she was the Sally Struthers of the organization, building a base of regular donors to sponsor the over one thousand children who now called the orphanage their home.

A couple of years later, my dad joined the university president on a trip to Cuernavaca for the orphanage's annual board meeting with its benefactors. My mom was helping organize the meeting, and my dad got the opportunity to get to know her over the course of the long weekend.

When my dad returned to South Carolina, he couldn't get her out of his mind. He knew almost immediately there was something special about my mom. He scheduled a meeting with his boss and requested to take a leave of absence to move to Mexico and help out at the orphanage. Soon my dad was packing for a year-long stay in Cuernavaca.

At the orphanage, as luck would have it, my dad was assigned to work in the sponsorship office alongside my mom. They started to casually date, but it was immediately obvious to him that my mom was more than just a fling. He fell in love with her sincere passion and heart for service.

Within a few months, my father became certain that my mom was the woman he was going to spend the rest of his life with. Even though he didn't have a ring, he couldn't wait any longer and asked her to marry him on a city bus while they were discussing their futures. Perhaps not the most romantic of proposals, but totally sincere. My mom said "yes," and they quietly started to make arrangements to return to the United States and start a life together.

Before they could begin planning a wedding, they told Father Wasson their plans to leave the orphanage. While he was sad to hear of their upcoming departure, he was excited that they had found such happiness in each other. He convinced them to get married in Cuernavaca, giving the children whom they had come to know and love an opportunity to witness the ceremony.

Just two weeks later, on a hot July day, my parents were married at the orphanage with Father Wasson presiding over the ceremony.

My mom continued to exemplify service to others throughout my life. One of my favorite memories from my upbringing was a time our family went out for dinner on Valentine's Day. While I don't remember what I ate or even the name of the restaurant, something so profound happened that the experience has stuck with my brother and me our entire lives and shaped the way I viewed public service.

As we looked at the menu and prepared to order, I noticed my mom glancing over at a woman dining alone three tables over. I was mid-sentence when my mom abruptly stood up and walked over to her table.

We couldn't hear what she said, but a few minutes later she returned to our table with a new friend.

"This is Pam,[38] and she is going to be joining us for dinner," my mother said.

Pam had special needs and used a wheelchair to get around. After their chance meeting at the restaurant, my mom and Pam became fast friends, regularly speaking on the phone and spending time with one another. My mom would help her run errands, take her to the movies, and invited her to spend Thanksgiving with our family.

Caring for a stranger in this way is an extraordinary gesture in our society. People tend to mind their own business and turn a blind eye to other people's problems, assuming someone else will take care of it.

To my mom, sitting on the sidelines when someone could use your help never occurred to her. In Pam, she saw someone who needed a friend and she stepped up to fill that role for no other reason than it was the right thing to do. Pam and my mom are still friends to this day.

This situation was not unique - my mom's heart for service has always permeated all aspects of her life. Community is more than gathering with friends. It is a calling to improve the lives of those around you, even complete strangers.

> Community is more than gathering with friends . It is a calling to improve the lives of those around you, even complete strangers.

Sometimes these acts of service were as simple as picking up someone else's litter in the parking lot on our walk into the grocery store. Other times they were much more elaborate, like the time she saw a woman carrying heavy groceries on the side of the road on a hot summer day. She stopped and gave her a ride home, then proceeded to raise money from around our neighborhood to buy a car for a woman she hardly knew, but for whom reliable transportation would prove to be life changing.

She never did any of these things for recognition or praise, attention, or glory. It came so naturally and so innately to her that that there simply was no other choice in her mind.

Caring for Your Community

While neither of my parents were political, they always modeled service and kindness to others. They understood that to make the world around you a better place, you must walk the walk when it comes to helping those in need within your community.

That help didn't have to be purely financial. Sometimes all it takes is a simple act of kindness to make someone's day and bring about a positive change in their life.

I recently asked my mom with her heart for service why she never ran for office. She responded that she was raised by a single mother who didn't have the time or energy to become invested in politics (other than she was convinced that Johnson killed Kennedy). Because it wasn't something that she grew up thinking or talking about, running for office never occurred to her. Plus, she was shy and lacked the self-confidence necessary for public speaking. Sounds familiar!

Women bring a unique sense of compassion and an innate ability to build community. I've often admired how stay-at-home moms possess incredible mental fortitude and calmness under pressure that tends to come from years of negotiating with toddlers - or as Caleb's grandfather calls them, "little dictators."

Studies on women in teams and in leadership roles have shown that their inclusion tends to lead to better decisions and more novel solutions. For example, a study of over 21,000 companies found that those that had 30% of their leadership positions filled by women were 15% more profitable than those without women on their boards or C-suites. Another study found that problem-solving teams with high social sensitivity, an attribute that women often bring to the table, outperformed others.

Male and female brains are motivated by different things in their decision-making processes. Men tend to take more risks in high-stress situations, motivated by a potentially big reward. Women tend to take more time weighing the options and are motivated by certainty, even if the payoff is smaller.[39]

Both strategies can be useful, depending on the situation. In order to ensure that the best policy decisions are being made, we need both men and women in the room.

Senator Rucker highlighted her own experience on how having a seat at the table impacted a policy debate in the West Virginia State Senate:

I bring a different perspective. Unlike most of the local elected officials, I'm not wealthy. My husband is a nurse.

We know what it's like to struggle. We know what it's like to not have money in our account at the end of the month. Because of that, I fight harder than a lot of legislators when they talk about raising taxes.

Recently, they wanted to raise the gas tax in order to raise money for road improvements. Now, everyone is in favor of better roads. I don't know anyone who is happy with the condition of their roads. But the way that some legislators were dismissing it – "it's only three cents a gallon" – was frustrating. For someone like myself, who is driving a minivan all over town because I have five kids, three cents a gallon adds up.

I live right on the border of West Virginia and Maryland, and if I can fill up on the other side of the border to save some money, I do. I was making these points in committee meetings. Not everyone can just absorb these increased costs. Some legislators just act like it's nothing, a penny here and a few cents there, but it adds up for families who are struggling.

There are only three female senators in the West Virginia Senate - out of 34. As you can imagine, in a lot of the committees that I'm on, I'm the only woman legislator. So, I do bring a different perspective than a man, and one that needs to be there. I do think I'm meant to be there, and I hope that I'm doing a good job of representing that viewpoint.

Senator Rucker brought something unique to the table in that discussion - the perspective of a busy mom. She also brought firsthand experience about how a policy change was going to affect not only her, but also tens of thousands of other families in West Virginia. And without her there, that critical perspective would have been completely left out of the conversation.

The Confidence Gap

Throughout American history, women like my mom have passionately and quietly been the glue that has kept our local communities together behind the scenes. History is filled with examples of strong women seeing a problem or injustice in their community and fighting to make a difference.

The problem is this desire rarely translates to political activism or running for office.

Women make up 50.8% of the population of the United States, but account for only 23.4% of the members of Congress. Even worse, Republican women make up less than 3% of Congress. This is the real gender gap we should care about!

> Women make up 50.8% of the population of the United States, but account for only 23.4% of the members of Congress. Even worse, Republican women make up less than 3% of Congress. This is the real gender gap we should care about!

While I believe we should always vote for the most qualified candidate who aligns with our values, regardless of gender, this poses a significant problem. Women and men are intrinsically different, and it is important for both sexes to have a seat at the table when discussing the critical issues our country is facing.

When talking to women about running for office, the most common response is a genuine laugh. They don't take the question seriously. It's never occurred to them. Even women who have been involved in politics as volunteers, as part of their local party, or as advocates in an organization, don't think of themselves when they think of who would make a good elected official.

More often than not, for women to run for office, it takes someone else who they trust and respect to ask them to consider running.

Lisa Nelson, Executive Director of the American Legislative Exchange Council, an influential organization of state legislators, mentioned this when we spoke.

> *There was an old stat: if you want a woman to run for office you have to ask her seven times, but if you want a man to run you only have to ask him once. Every woman I have ever known who has run has taken a long time to decide because they have to consider how it impacts their families, their relationships, their jobs, etc. I think that's a natural thing, but I'm really heartened to see on the left and on the right of more women getting involved, more women feeling comfortable in the role, more women feeling empowered.*

When women are pressed to consider running, all of the practical reasons to say "no" come to mind. But beyond that, there is a common hesitation that seems to be pervasive: they don't think of themselves as qualified. Fiercely smart, imminently capable, and truly inspiring women for some reason do not believe that they have the right credentials or background or knowledge of the issues.

Senator Susan Collins from Maine has noticed the same thing. She was quoted in a 2016 New York Times article titled "The Problem for Women Is Not Winning. It's Deciding to Run" saying, "I have never ever had a male potential candidate say to me that he wasn't ready, that he didn't feel prepared enough. Over and over again, I have had potential female candidates say to me that they just don't feel they're quite ready, that they need more experience."[40]

> A growing body of evidence consistently shows that women and men are separated by a vast "confidence gap." Men tend to overestimate their abilities. Women are more prone to doubt their abilities and performance, eve n when their results are equal to men's.

A growing body of evidence consistently shows that women and men are separated by a vast "confidence gap." Men tend to overestimate their abilities and have more confidence in their performance, which in turn causes them to take more risks and pursue more leadership roles. Meanwhile, women are more prone to doubt their abilities and performance, even when their results are equal to men's. This makes them less likely to think of themselves as qualified. This low confidence leads to inaction and hesitation to apply for a job, ask for a raise, or run for office.

The confidence gap has been demonstrated in many studies like the one below:

> One often-cited study found that when men and women performed equally on a science test, women thought they performed worse, and were less likely to enter a science competition as a result.

> (A) survey of college students . . . found that men were twice as likely to say they would be qualified to run for office after graduating and working for a while, while women were 20 percentage points more likely to say they would not be. Part of the reason is that society rewards men for ambition, but not necessarily women, and women are socialized to be hesitant about promoting themselves.

This issue continues throughout our lives.

When Hewlett-Packard set out to get more women into management positions, they reviewed their personnel records. What they found was that women typically applied for a promotion only after they met 100 percent of the qualifications listed in the job posting. Men, on the other hand, applied when they met about 60 percent of the criteria necessary for the job. Men's confidence, regardless of their ability, propels them to success. Meanwhile, women are holding themselves back and forgoing opportunities in pursuit of perfection.[41]

While there are practical and logistical considerations to take into account when deciding to run for office, not feeling qualified is a myth that must be done away with completely.

This message needs to be heard loud and clear: there is no special criteria necessary in order to as a spokesperson for a cause, a leader of a movement, or an elected official. You don't need to be an expert in every policy area, you don't need to have a degree in political science or law, you don't need to be well-connected, and you don't need a lot of money.

All you need is your 'why' - an issue that you really care about - and an opportunity to make an impact. And then you need to act, without overanalyzing all of the reasons that would otherwise hold you back.

> There is no special criteria necessary in order to serve as a spokesperson for a cause, a leader of a movement, or an elected official. You don't need to be an expert in every policy area, you don't need to have a degree in political science or law, you don't need to be well-connected, and you don't need a lot of money. All you need is your 'why' - an issue that you really care about - and an opportunity to make an impact.

We put our elected officials up on a pedestal with a certain air of awe and respect that makes the position seem unattainable. But in reality, every single elected official in this country, with the exception of a certain few who were born into a family of political tradition, was just a regular person like you or me before they ran for office. We do not live in a monarchy. Political service is for anyone who has a calling to make the world around them better.

Rarely do I see this hesitation and lack of confidence in men. As one of the few conservatives in Austin to have attained public office, men frequently reach out to me for advice on launching a campaign. I always ask them why they want to run, and the answers I get back do not lack confidence. Instead, they are more along the lines of "I'm interested in public policy, and I think I'd be good at it" and "It's something I have always wanted to do, and I have a lot to offer."

While sitting in a local coffee shop one day with someone who was seeking my advice about potentially running for office, I asked him why he thought we don't have more women active in politics and he said, "I don't know, I think they are just less interested." My eyeroll that followed was likely hard to miss.

Generally, men don't express doubt about their capabilities when considering whether to run for office. Not to say they don't have their own challenges to consider, but this idea of not being qualified seems to be unique to women. A National Public Radio segment from 2014 titled "Best Way to Get Women to Run for Office? Ask Repeatedly" highlighted this same issue.[42]

> When Monica Youngblood got the call, she thought it was a joke. The call came from a man she had worked to help get elected.
>
> "It's your time," she says he told her. "We need people like you in Santa Fe. We need a voice like yours who's lived

here, who's been through what you've been through. I think you need to really consider it."

When she realized it wasn't a joke, Youngblood had a lot of questions — and self-doubt.

"Thoughts from, 'Am I qualified to do this? Do we have the time?'' she says. "It will be a sacrifice, not only to my profession but my family, my kids."

Youngblood is now a Republican representing Albuquerque, N.M., in the State House of Representatives. When she got that call, she was a mother and real estate agent who had been volunteering on other people's campaigns for about a decade.

This initial reluctance is common among female candidates, according to Sue Ellspermann, Indiana's lieutenant governor.

'When they asked me to consider running, I said, 'Oh no. I haven't run for anything since high school student council,'" Ellspermann says. "So they said, 'Oh, just think about it.'"

Ellspermann has a Ph.D. in industrial engineering and owned her own business. Yet she was convinced she wasn't qualified. Brenda Major, a social psychologist at the University of California, Santa Barbara, isn't surprised.

"It makes sense, given what we know about women and confidence and self-confidence," Major says.

Her research finds that women have less confidence in their own abilities, judge themselves harshly — even when they are successful — and carry failures as more of a burden than men do.

"So many competent, capable women are basically select-ing themselves out of leadership positions and I think that we've all wrestled with this," Major says. "I know it per-sonally. I know it firsthand."

This has to be addressed if we want to increase the number of women running for and serving in our elected bodies.

No matter where they fall on the political spectrum, women generally run for office because they are motivated by a decision or event that made them mad and they became determined to change. I have yet to meet a woman motivated to run for office because it is "something that she has always wanted to do."

For a woman to decide to run for office, it tends to be less about fulfilling a personal ambition or believing that they offer something that others can't, and more about addressing a partic-ular issue that is motivating them.

That is not to say that men don't run for office for the right reasons and women do. I have been privileged to know many honorable and dedicated men in Texas politics who care deeply about their constituents and have a genuine heart for service. In fact, without the support and encouragement of my mentors and friends, many of whom are men, I may never have run for office myself. Many of the women who share their stories in this book had similar experiences.

The point is that while men generally have the confidence to run for office when they feel they could make a difference or simply because they've always wanted to, it often takes a specific event to serve as a catalyst for a woman to run. Maybe their child came home from school one day reciting a controversial political opinion taught by their teacher as fact, the local city council wasted taxpayer dollars on a mismanaged city project, or even just their property taxes this year were too high. But we don't have the luxury to wait around for those inciting incidents. This mindset must be changed if we want to see more women run for office.

Say "Yes"

Was it easy for me to run for city council in the most liberal city in Texas? No, it was one of the most difficult things I have ever done. But it was also one of the most rewarding.

Was it easy for me to balance the needs of my family and the growth of my business with my dedication to improving the lives of my constituents? Absolutely not. But the hard work paid off, and I ultimately completed my service knowing unequivocally that the people who called my city home were better off because of my involvement.

I was successful, not because I am special, but because I didn't let fear or doubt get in the way of taking action.

Do you loathe the direction our country is moving? Do you have unique ideas that could solve the government's most vexing problems? Do you find yourself turning off the news out of frustration because you are sick and tired of rhetoric not matching results?

By not getting involved you are not only denying yourself, but you are denying your children, your neighbors, and future generations of your unique contributions to the world. Don't let anyone tell you that you can't make a difference. You can! Will you?

We can't win this battle by posting on social media or listening to talk radio. These things won't move the needle. Only more conservative women running for and getting elected to public office will make a difference.

We can't win this battle by posting on social media or listening to talk radio. These things won't move the needle. Only more conservative women running for and get elected to public office will make a difference.

When I discussed the outlook of electing more conservative women in the next election with Congresswoman McMorris Rodgers, she seemed very optimistic:

I have never been more encouraged than I am right now. Know that you are not alone, although the media wants you to feel like that. 2018 was tough and the Democrats targeted nearly all of the Republican women in the House and we lost several of our women who were good friends of mine.

However, just a couple weeks after, I sat down with a woman I have known for many years. We have worked together on disability issues, and I thought that was what the lunch was about. I was still kind of in the depths of despair, wondering where this was headed. She said 'Cathy, I want to run for Congress,' and I could have fallen off my seat. This was November of 2018, and it is not a pretty picture for conservative women in Congress. She says, 'I want to run for Congress in Kansas.' And I thought, 'Wow, that's awesome.' She was ready to get in the ring, and she recognized it was going to be a fight, but it was a fight worth having. And it has just continued ever since then.

I am meeting with women nearly every week who want to run, and this has been going on for over a year. We have over 200 women now from districts representing probably every state that have contacted National Republican Congressional Committee and said, 'I'm interested in running for Congress.'

For so many years, I was recruiting women in different communities who were leaders or had been serving in office and talking to them about running for Congress. They were so quick to tell me why they weren't the one. Whatever it was, if it was family or community, they were very quick to give me a reason as to why they were not the one. And yet, now, I'm seeing more women that are saying 'you know what, I do have something to offer and my country needs people to step up and run.'

Women need role models and be able to look to other women and say, 'She did it, I can do it.' That is important. And we need to encourage each other. We need to encourage women in our communities who we think are doing a great job to consider some of these positions.

Conservative women exist in bigger numbers and harbor more frustration than the media or your local city council would lead you to believe, and there is power in those numbers. But in order to win, we must mobilize.

KEY INSIGHTS

- Women already serve as the glue that holds our communities together, volunteering at their children's schools, serving at their churches, and caring for their neighbors.
- That compassion, along with the problem-solving skills that are unique to women, is desperately needed in our legislative bodies as well.
- Women suffer from a well-documented "confidence gap" that causes them to underestimate their skills and performance, making them less likely to take action.
- Women often have to be asked repeatedly by others to run for office to overcome the confidence gap. There are no special qualifications or degrees necessary to run, just a willingness to take action.
- We are seeing more women step up than ever before. Be a part of it!

CALL TO ACTION

They're lying! Who? The voices in your head that express doubt about your abilities. Overcome the confidence gap by believing in yourself and encouraging the women around you. Apply for the job promotion, raise your hand for the leadership position, support your friend's passion projects, and get off the sidelines and onto the field in policy and politics. The only thing holding you back is your hesitancy to act. We need *you*, and you've got this!

5

The Case for Men to Care

If I got my heart for service from my mom, I got my work ethic and optimism from my dad.

My dad is a genuine embodiment of the American Dream. Like many young families, when my parents first had children, paying the bills was a real struggle each month. They always made it work, but I am sure there were times when it was stressful.

Over time, my dad's hard work and perseverance paid off, and he was able to advance in his career and make enough money to provide a comfortable life for our family. We were never rich, but we always had what we needed.

My dad has a warm spirit, and he always seeks to build other people up. It was almost like growing up with a motivational speaker for a father. He is a habitual optimist and took pride in everything he did, no matter how menial it might seem.

To this day when doing chores around the house, I hear a chorus in my head of "*Ellen, finish the job.*" Anytime I vacuumed but didn't shake the rugs out, I would get the "finish the job" lecture. To my dad, it was always important to finish what you started, and do it well, rather than leave an incomplete job for later, or for someone else to take care of. While I appreciate this advice now, I didn't have the same appreciation for his life lessons as a teenager.

Characteristically, my dad would weave motivational quotes into discussion as teaching tools all the time. If I expressed doubt in something, he would often quote Henry Ford: "*If you think you can, or you think you can't, you are probably right.*"

My dad also has a personal motto. I can still quote it off the top of my head: grow tirelessly, share endlessly, love unconditionally, and serve selflessly.

That motto sums up my parents and the values I was raised on. I was lucky enough to have two parents who provided a stable and supportive childhood. It was important to my dad to raise a smart, capable, compassionate daughter. I hope my children learn similar life lessons from me.

Most men value the women in their lives, just like my dad. They have moms, wives, and daughters who they love, respect, and want only the best for. So, encouraging more women to get involved in politics isn't an issue of promoting women at the expense of men, it is about ensuring we have both perspectives at the table. In my experience, men are very supportive of this notion.

A couple months back, I had the opportunity to attend a small luncheon featuring a well-respected congresswoman. After her remarks, a discussion broke out about what we can do to get more women elected to public office, focusing on barriers, solutions, ideas, and advice to women interested in serving their communities.

While young women made up a sizeable chunk of the audience, in the midst of the discussion, I realized something - half of the audience was made up of influential older men. As if reading my mind, the organizer observed with humor that this was likely the first time any of these men had been involved in a conversation like that. And you know what? I bet she was right.

While it is important for women to be having conversations with one another about running for office and getting involved in the political process, it is important that we don't leave men out of the discussion.

While it is important for women to be having conversations with one another about running for office and getting involved in the political process, it is important that we don't leave men out of the discussion. Men not only make up half of the population, but they make up a huge majority of the current body of elected officials. This means we can utilize their enthusiasm and institutional knowledge to encourage women to join their ranks and get involved.

However, to get men interested and invested, they have to be made generally aware that the problem exists. To do this, we must have an open dialogue about the gender gap in politics and why it is important to address, not only for their wives and daughters but for the future of our country.

Men understand the value that women bring to our communities and governments. There are lots of incredibly supportive husbands who serve as true partners in their marriages, shouldering their share of the household and financial burdens, making it easier for their wives to pursue their personal or professional goals. There are plenty of fathers who make raising their children a priority and want their daughters to know that they can become anything they want to be.

These men can be incredibly helpful in raising the issue into the public consciousness.

In the tribal world we currently live in, it may seem hard to believe that men will care, because on the surface it seems it does not affect them. But the reality is, that a lack of conservative women serving in leadership roles, especially as elected officials, is impacting men and women alike in diversity of thought, public policy outcomes, and electorally.

What Women Bring to the Table Electorally

A lack of women running for public office poses a significant problem for Republicans electorally. In just twelve years, women went from voting 48% for George W. Bush in 2004, to only 41% supporting Donald Trump in 2016. A recent Pew Research poll showed that 48% of men think there are too few women in political offices, compared to 69% of women who share this view.[43]

Another recent survey showed that roughly one-third of young women would prefer voting for a woman over a man.[44] In the 2018 midterms, Democrats capitalized on these sentiments, running 356 women for Congress, up 166 candidates from their previous record in 2012. Meanwhile, only 120 Republican women ran for Congress, down from their high mark of 128 in 2010.[45] Women were the nominees in 42% of House races for the Democrats, while women made up only 12% of nominees for Republicans.[46] It is no wonder they were successful in taking back the majority in Congress.

> A recent survey showed that roughly one-third of young women would prefer voting for a woman over a man. In the 2018 midterms, Democrats capitalized on these sentiments, running 356 women for congress, up 166 candidates from their previous record in 2012. Meanwhile, only 120 Republican women ran for Congress, down from their high mark of 128 in 2010. Women were the nominees in 42% of House races for the Democrats, while women made up only 12% of nominees for Republicans. It is no wonder they were successful in taking back the majority in Congress.

While I don't defend divisive identity politics when used as a way to judge someone based solely on their gender or race, a lack of diversity is a legitimate problem for the Republican Party. By spending time and resources electing women and minorities, the Democrats have been able to mobilize and influence new voters, creating diverse coalitions of support for enacting large-scale societal changes that would have seemed impossible just a decade ago.

You have to hand it to them: the Democrats have made this a priority and have truly put their money where their mouth is. For example, EMILY'S List, a political action committee that works to elect pro-choice Democrat women, spent nearly $10 million in the 2018 campaign cycle alone. Ten million dollars in one campaign cycle![47]

During that same election, Run for Something, a PAC that supports millennial liberal candidates with the intention of building a bench of future candidates, aimed to raise $3 million.[48]

Like it or not, people are more prone to vote for candidates with whom they can relate and identify. This means Republicans have to do a better job of running candidates who look and sound like the populations they are seeking to represent. This isn't rocket science; it's just human nature. We tend to connect with people who have similar life experiences.

Randan Steinhauser, public relations and political communications strategist, underscores this point while discussing how women are reshaping politics, "Candidate recruitment is so important. Women don't only vote for women, but they respond best to a messenger who can relate and talk about the issues that are important to them."[49]

As conservatives, we like to believe that you should only vote for people based on their values and policy perspectives, regardless of their race or gender. However, we are not losing traditional conservatives; we are losing casual voters who share many of our values but feel Republicans don't care about their community because the people we are electing form a homogenous group that lacks age, gender, and racial diversity.

We don't need to change our message; we need to diversify our messengers.

By not nominating candidates who are more representative of our society as a whole, we are missing out on perspectives and life experiences that could add richness to our political dialogue and help open up lines of communication to demographics that currently have no interest in voting Republican.

We don't need to change our message; we need to diversify our messengers.

In this vein, the story of Alexandria Ocasio-Cortez is one that we can learn from. In June of 2018, Congressman Joe Crowley had served in Congress for twenty years, was Chair of the House Democratic Caucus, and was considered one of the most powerful individuals in Washington, D.C.

On the night of the Democratic Primary in New York, if you would have told any reputable political analyst that Congressman Crowley would be defeated by a twenty-nine-year-old socialist bartender from the Bronx, they would have laughed in your face. And yet, on June 26, 2018, Alexandria Ocasio-Cortez not only defeated Crowley, but won with 57% of the vote.

After the election of President Trump, the far-left has seen a revival much like the far-right had after the election of President Obama. Similar to how the Tea Party sought to bring new blood into the Republican Party and elect more liberty-minded, populist candidates to office, groups like Justice Democrats are fighting to unseat moderate incumbent Democrats and replace them with leftists more aligned with Senator Bernie Sanders.

Sean McElwee, a prominent liberal pollster, has referred to these clashes as "ideological contests for the soul of the Democratic Party."[50]

The election of Ocasio-Cortez (AOC) was essentially the crown jewel of the 2018 midterms for Justice Democrats. While their success rate was low, electing the prominent firebrand of AOC has reinvigorated the group and given it the attention and resources necessary to be more relevant in 2020.

The importance of relevance isn't lost on AOC. Since her election, she has capitalized on her unique position to become the de facto spokesperson for the far-left and has literally shifted the dialogue around what the major issues will be for the Democratic Party leading up to 2020 presidential primary.

To see a real-life example of this, you don't have to look any further than the issue of climate change. While few Democrat candidates will admit to being skeptical about climate change, typically environmentalism has been relegated to a bullet point on a campaign website, not a focal point of the party platform.

That all changed with AOC and the Green New Deal. Now, virtually every Democrat contender for the White House has their own plan to address climate change. CNN even hosted a seven-hour-long town hall forum dedicated solely to the issue of climate change and the environment.

Often, success in politics isn't necessarily about having the right message but having the right messenger.

AOC has taken some pretty radical stances, but she has done so with a populist flair. While a majority of Americans probably would not support her socialist-leaning economic positions, she sells them by stating: *"The working class aren't asking for a lot. They are just trying to get by, and they are asking their elected officials to help them get by."*[51] This sounds reasonable, until you understand the way in which she hopes to accomplish this vision.

As conservatives, we often think having a consistent voting record based on an air-tight ideological philosophy will get more voters to the polls. That might be the case for grassroots activists during a primary, but for many casual general election voters, tone, style, appearance, and likeability of the candidate play a much larger role.

AOC succeeds, not because of what she says, but because her delivery is bold, and she isn't straddling both sides of issues. She's an effective communicator and persuader in part because of her authenticity.

Public Policy Outcomes

Increasing the diversity of our ballot and having the right messenger won't just help us electorally; it will help us in public policy battles in state legislatures and Congress.

Like it or not, the media attack men like sharks when they speak about and debate social issues. How many times have you heard pundits complain that "men have no right to tell a woman what's right for their body," "her body, her choice," or even that "women should have 100% control over their own reproductive decisions"?

The optics on pro-life legislation improve drastically when women are authoring and supporting the bill.

Take, for example, the national outcry over the passage of Alabama's "The Human Life Protection Act." Although 58% of Alabama citizens,[52] including 51% of women, thought abortion should be illegal in all or most cases, the narrative became that men were trying to take away the rights of the women they represent.

In fact, a USA Today article's headline read: "25 men voted to ban abortion in Alabama. Do they reflect the rest of America?[53]"

Set aside the fact that the rest of the country's opinion should have no bearing on the laws passed by an individual state - do you think that headline would have worked if the Alabama legislature had more women in the chamber?

In 2013, when former Texas Senator Wendy Davis made a national name for herself, filibustering legislation that would prohibit the abortion of a child after twenty weeks, Senator Leticia Van De Putte scolded then-Lt. Governor David Dewhurst, asking: *"At what point must a female senator raise her hand or her voice to be recognized over her male colleagues?"[54]*

Do you think her point would have been as impactful if the Lt. Governor had been a woman? Conservatives often have the right message, but we far too often fail to take into account the importance of the person delivering it.

For women reading this, it is time to step up and run for public office or take the next step into a leadership role within your community or organization.

For men, this is also an opportunity to speak up in support of women's involvement in the political process. The confidence gap discussed in the previous chapter means that women tend to underestimate their skills and abilities compared to their actual performance.

Because women often need external encouragement to realize that they could be the best spokesperson for an issue, leader of a cause, or candidate for office, look for opportunities to provide that encouragement.

> Knowing that women often need an external encouragement for them to realize that they could be the best spokesperson for an issue, leader of a cause, or candidate for office, look for opportunities to provide that encouragement.

Many of the women who share their stories in this book were initially approached about running for office by a man who believed in them and may not be where they are today without that support. While my hope is that this reality will eventually change, in the meantime, helping the sharp and capable women you know overcome their own doubts will go a long way.

KEY INSIGHTS

- The gender gap in politics matters to men too! We all benefit from having good role models for our daughters and sons.
- People like voting for women. A lack of diversity on the ballot is undermining our ability to elect leaders who support conservative values that both men and women care about.
- The Left understands that having the right messenger allows them to reach more people and make a better case for policies they support. We must do the same.
- Men are a critical part of helping women overcome the confidence gap, but they have to be made aware of the problem to help.

CALL TO ACTION

Talk to your husband, your boyfriend, or your male friends about the disparity of women in politics and why it matters. Hand them this book and ask them to read (at least) this chapter. Then discuss what they can do to support you, and other women you know, in your efforts.

PART TWO

THE PLAYBOOK

6
How to Advocate

Since 1935, Gallup has been measuring public opinion on issues and political institutions to see how people feel about their government and the world around them. Gallup describes itself as having "built its reputation on delivering relevant, timely, and visionary research on what humans around the world think and feel."[55]

Since 1974, Gallup has included the following question in its polling and tracked it over time: "Do you approve or disapprove of the way Congress is handling its job?"

Over the years, the approval ratings of Congress have dropped lower and lower. Between 2010-2018, Congress's approval rating exceeded 20% only 24 times (out of 96 months). During that same period, Congress's approval rating never reached 30%.[56]

Interestingly, while the Gallup poll does not ask the question as frequently, when asked: "Do you approve or disapprove of the way the representative from your congressional district is handling his or her job?", people overwhelmingly support their own congressperson, with support never dipping below 40% and often hovering in the 50-60% range.

People tend to like the people they elect to represent themselves, while despising the people everyone else elects. People inherently know there is power in supporting their elected leaders, but rarely ever think to contact their elected officials and use it.

Knowing the System

As a former city elected official and state legislative staffer, I can tell you firsthand that very few people contact the officials who represent them, especially at the local or state level. Most people vote and end their participation there - if they even vote.

There is a lot of time spent in the offices of state capitols explaining to constituents that it is not the same as the office of their Congressman or woman in Washington, D.C. Most people are busy and don't have time to learn the intricacies of how the various levels of government work, what their jurisdictions are, what issues they deal with, or even who represents them at what level of government.

In order to beat the system, you have to know the system. You can't effectively participate in the game, if you don't know the rules. Here's a quick primer.

The systems of government vary depending on the city or state that you live in. It's important to understand the fundamentals of how those systems are set up where you live. Local elected bodies generally include the city council, the county commissioners court, and the school board. But you may have different terminology, and it can be confusing! For example, Texas' counties are governed by a Commissioners Court. In California, the body that oversees the county is called the Board of Supervisors.

To make matters worse, boundary lines of the different jurisdictions are rarely the same. They zig and zag in an unpredictable manner that can change depending on which side of the street you're on. Your city might span multiple counties and your county might include multiple school districts.

The good thing is that most of this information is easily accessible through a quick internet search. You should be able to find information about who represents you, the district lines, the length of the terms, and other basic criteria on the website of the entity.

Another useful tip is to take a close look at your property tax bill. It likely lists the taxing jurisdictions. If there is a tax levied, there is probably some kind of elected body that is setting those rates. You may be surprised to find things like special utility districts, community college districts, health districts, and other bodies that you could run for or possibly be appointed to.

> Take a close look at your property tax bill. It likely lists the taxing jurisdictions. If there is a tax levied, there is probably some kind of elected body that is setting those rates. You may be surprised to find things like special utility districts, community college districts, health districts, and other bodies that you could run for or possibly be appointed to.

Once you have this information, you should understand the issues that they each have jurisdiction over. The school board collect taxes and sets the budget and programming for your local schools. While individual campuses will vary in the details, the district-wide decisions like school boundaries, curriculum, and administration are set by the school board. Similarly, the city sets the tax rate and allocates money to city programs, like police officers, health and human services, and parks and libraries. They also control zoning and permitting for buildings. The county often has control over things like the local court system and the jail, as well as road infrastructure and ordinances governing things like noise and light outside the city limits.

While this may sound overwhelming, just taking a few minutes to familiarize yourself with the governments that were created to serve you is extremely powerful. Often times, these bodies have the lowest turnout in elections, which means they also have the least oversight. Not only does every vote in these elections make a difference, but you can also educate and influence your friends. Being even minimally informed will put you ahead of the curve.

Here are some basic questions you'll want to answer:
- Who represents me?
- What are the district boundaries?
- How long are the terms?
- What issues do they have jurisdiction over?

Becoming generally familiar with this information is powerful. If you don't know who is making decisions on your behalf, how can you expect them to know how to best represent you?

The next step is to make sure your elected officials know who you are. If you are one of the few people who care enough to reach out to your legislator, you have an amplified voice to get things done.

Interacting with Your Elected Officials

There is power in reaching out to your elected official. When an office receives a few dozen letters or calls from constituents on an issue, it will certainly prompt a discussion about the issue. The more correspondence they receive about a subject, the higher up it is on their radar and their list of things to address.

Most elected officials enter office with a set of core beliefs that they will not violate, but there are many other issues are not the passionate partisan ones you hear about on TV. As a result, the perspective of constituents plays a heavy hand in not only making decisions on how to vote on these types of issues, but which to prioritize and bring up for a vote.

Don't just take my word for it. I reached out to State Representative Julie Emerson of Louisiana to talk about her campaign for public office and her thoughts about serving. Elected at age 27, Emerson is the youngest person in the Louisiana Legislature. When I asked her about what citizens can do to have a stronger voice at their state Capitol, she had some great insight.

*People just want to know that their representative will lis-
ten to them and are accessible. That is why I always do my
best to return my phone calls within a day or so. If there's
a constituent in my district who wants to meet with me, I
always make time to meet with them.*

*I've toured a lot of businesses and I met with tons of people
on nights or weekends. I hope that the people in my district
understand that I'm genuine about wanting to represent
them. A lot of times when you get angry constituent emails
or phone calls, if you respond and ask if they want to sit
down and talk in person, it really disarms them.*

*A lot of people think that elected officials are influenced
by big corporations or lobbyists, but I'm telling you, there
is nothing that puts the fear in powerful legislators like
having 300 constituent emails come in about some bill or
issue. They will flip immediately.*

*I've heard it a thousand times from my colleagues: 'People
in my district don't want this, I can't vote for this!" Legislators may not be able to respond to every single email
individually, but they do see them. It does matter. They
know that their inbox is getting flooded about some bill and
it absolutely makes a difference.'*

Constituents being involved in the legislative process can go
further than just impacting votes; they can actually impact the
legislation that is being introduced for consideration.

Eve Wiley of Dallas experienced this firsthand in 2019 when
she successfully advocated and lobbied to pass legislation to crim-
inalize fertility fraud. The story is heartbreaking, but is a great
testament of what you can get done if you step up and advocate
to your elected leaders:

Wiley said Williams [her mother] and her late husband, a schoolteacher who died of cardiomyopathy when Eve was 7, struggled with infertility before finally deciding to use a sperm donation from California Cryobank. That's how Eve was conceived.

With her awareness of the importance of medical history raised by her late husband's heart problem, Williams sought more genetic and health care information about Sperm Donor No. 106, Eve's presumed father. That left a trove of emails in her mother's computer, Wiley said.

"When I was 16 — my mother's a school nurse — I was going through her emails trying to get some juicy gossip on my cohorts," she testified. "And I stumbled upon the correspondence that she had with California Cryobank and learned that I was the juicy gossip. That's how I found out I was donor-conceived."

Wiley soon developed a "father-daughter relationship" with Donor No. 106, she recounted.

"I call him dad. We say I love you," Wiley said. "We spend holidays together and he actually officiated at my wedding."[57]

Unfortunately, in 2018, everything changed. Wiley had genetic testing done on 23andMe.com and Ancestry.com and found out that her father was not Donor No. 106 but was instead a man by the name of Dr. Kim McMorries - the doctor who conducted the procedure.

Wiley said she was stricken. "So my mother's fertility doctor decided to use his own sperm instead of the sperm do-

nor that my parents selected and consented to, and without their knowledge," she testified. "And then I had to be the one to tell my mother that this had happened." Telling [donor] No. 106, who she had come to know as her father, also was emotionally wrenching, she said.

Worse yet, Wiley discovered after speaking with an attorney that there were no provisions in Texas law that made such action illegal.

She decided to engage in the legislative process. Soon she had a bill drafted and an author identified to shepherd it through the legislative process. Throughout the legislative session, Wiley traveled to Austin and frequently shared her story with legislators and staff.

Although the bill was filed late in the game, it quickly began moving and passed the state senate about a month after its introduction. Word about her story quickly spread throughout the Texas Capitol, stories were written in the Dallas Morning News, and she was even featured on ABC's 20/20.

The bill passed the House in mid-May and was signed by the governor shortly after. Because Wiley cared enough to pursue change and was brave enough to share her story with the legislature and the general public, Texas unanimously passed the toughest fertility fraud legislation in the nation. If a doctor gets caught using sperm from an unauthorized donor, it is now considered sexual assault, and those found guilty must register as sex offenders.

Not all bills being considered by the legislature are as heavy and emotional as the one described above. Few people ever pass the huge, controversial bills that garner a lot of public attention, but for the most part, every legislator passes something each session.

As a result, legislators are always looking for small, local victories they can tout back home when they are on the campaign trail. This means, if you see a small problem in your community that could use corrective action, there is a chance your representative will go to bat and try to have it addressed through legislation.

When I was a senior in college, I was an intern at the Texas Capitol for State Representative Phil King. I worked part-time in between my classes at the University of Texas and made $400 per month. While it wasn't a lot of money, I was just excited to be a part of the process.

Each day was a new adventure, and I was constantly surprised at the vast array of issues that came across my small, shared desk. One day, a sheriff from my boss's district called about an issue with the local dog catcher. That's right, the dog catcher. The lack of any education for animal control officers was causing problems in their local community. I took down the details and later discussed it with Representative King.

"Does this sound like something we could and should find a solution for legislatively?" he asked me.

"I think so?" I answered, hesitantly.

"If I file a bill, would you like to be the point person for it?" he questioned.

Keep in mind that I was an intern. I answered the phones and got the mail. I had picked up some knowledge during the time I worked at the Capitol, but I knew more about what kind of coffee the Representative liked than how to pass a bill.

Nevertheless, I enthusiastically said, "Sure! I'd love to!"

And I did. Over the next few months, I worked with stakeholders from animal advocates to local law enforcement to craft a bill that would address the problem. With help from our Legislative Director, a handsome guy named Caleb (whom I later married), I somehow helped Representative King usher legislation through both the House and Senate committees, onto the calendar, through both chambers, and onto the Governor's desk for signature.

There are literally thousands of bills filed every session in the Texas Legislature. Only a small fraction of them become law, especially in the first session they are filed. We had done it, and it felt awesome! It blew my mind that a college student with an accidental interest in politics had been instrumental in changing the law for the State of Texas.

While it's easy to be cynical about politics, I had seen the process work firsthand and was amazed that someone who simply saw a problem or had a good idea could change the law. All they had to do was care enough to reach out to their elected representative and ask. If I, a college intern, could do it, anyone could do it.

And all it takes is a phone call or meeting with your elected official to see what's possible.

Contacting Your Elected Officials

Simply reaching out to your elected officials can make a huge difference in moving the ball forward for issues you are passionate about. While all forms of communication are useful, some are more impactful than others and will leave a lasting impression on the mind of the officials and their staff.

In-Person Meeting

By far the most effective way of communicating with your elected official is through a personal meeting. This could take place in their district or capitol office, a local coffee shop, or after a local event. Regardless of the location, if you live in the district, the odds are your representative will meet with you and at least hear you out.

The most important thing is simply to show up and make that in-person connection. Because very few people take the time to do this, your effort to introduce yourself will be memorable. If you want to discuss a specific topic, try

> By far the most effective way of communicating with your elected official is through a personal meeting. Try to present a tangible way to solve a problem rather than just discussing your thoughts on a general issue.

to come to the meeting prepared with evidence for your cause. Consider putting together a one-page document outlining the key points in order to ensure your representative retains the information you spoke about and has something to pass along to their staff to follow up on. Try to present a tangible way to solve a problem rather than just discussing your thoughts on a general issue.

Phone Call

If you can't make an in-person meeting, do not hesitate to call their office. The odds are you will end up speaking with a member of their staff, but staff does most of the day-to-day work anyway and can be a good advocate for you to their boss.

Especially during contentious votes, staff field a lot of calls. To be impactful and stand out, always be respectful and refrain from using colorful language that could leave a bad impression or make them feel uncomfortable. If you are upset about a political issue, even a vote taken by your elected representative, don't take it out on the staff member.

Instead, try to include personal anecdotes to demonstrate your passion and why this issue is so meaningful to you. My staff were often moved by the testimony they heard over the phones and would relay messages to me that helped me better serve the people I was blessed to represent.

Physical Letters & Emails

Sending a letter or an email to your elected official allows you to succinctly put your thoughts to paper and provide supporting evidence for what you want done. This ensures that the message you want delivered is not lost in translation by leaving a message with staff over the phone. Sometimes the best strategy is to call, have a discussion, and then send an email or letter as follow-up.

Elected officials get a lot of letters, and as a result, many utilize pre-written templates for their responses, especially if you just write them about a broad issue like protecting the Second Amendment or lowering taxes. If the response you receive seems canned and you want more specifics, I recommend picking up the phone or scheduling a meeting.

Form Letters

If you are on an email list for an advocacy group or think tank, many times they will send you a link to sign a form letter to your elected officials on various issues. Elected officials and their staff are fully aware that these are pre-written letters. If it is customizable, always make it your own so it stands out. If you don't have time, that is okay too. At a minimum, it will increase the tally in favor of your stance on an issue in their constituent correspondence database.

Social Media

While it may not be the best way to start a dialogue with your elected officials, social media is a great way to increase pressure on them. If they get a lot of comments or tweets about a specific issue or position on a public platform, they may feel more urgency to act. Being respectful and productive is always the best way to promote action. While some people are more emboldened when they can hide behind a keyboard, using offensive language, disparaging the official, or being a troll is never a productive strategy. The goal is change, not "likes."

Advocating for an Issue at the Capitol or City Hall

Many organizations, whether it is a professional association or issue-based advocacy organization, host advocacy days at the capitol or city hall in order to show support for their policy priorities. Attending these days is a great way to get a feel for the political scene and meet your representatives while having someone else do the legwork. They will often schedule the meetings with your elected officials, provide the handouts, and prepare you for the day.

For the most part, elected officials appreciate the thoughts and concerns raised by their constituents. You just have to know to ask for a meeting, and at that meeting be prepared with talking points and a direct ask.

As former New Mexico State Representative-turned-Congressional candidate Yvette Herrell said, you don't have to be an expert to participate, just share your viewpoints and experience.

> *The point of government, especially on the state representative level, but even the Congressional level . . . is to represent the people. What a novel idea, right?*
>
> *And when somebody gets up there [in office] and they know better than the guy making the payroll every week, or the woman who sends her children to public school . . . when people decide that they know better than the people who put him in office then shame on them. Then it's time for them to go.*

I'm versed in issues . . . But you need to make the call to somebody at those construction companies, medical facilities, and mom and pop businesses and say what does this [legislation] look like.

Your feedback on the issue that you have firsthand experience with or expertise in is essential to the policymaking process. Legislators will be able to come up with better policy solutions if they have your input.

Most of your elected officials welcome your feedback and would be glad to utilize your expertise as they sort through the challenges presented before them. You just have to step up, establish these relationships, and share what you know!

Getting Involved

While legislators value the ideas, concerns, and opinions of all of their constituents, they each have certain constituents who carry more pull than others. These tend to be community or grassroots leaders that have a large influence in their local area and have the ability to mobilize in a way that can help or harm them in their next re-election campaign.

Elected officials know who runs their local Republican clubs, who writes the big checks, and who can get together a large group on a Saturday to knock on doors and make phone calls. They value these people and will go out of their way to make sure they are aware of their opinions and concerns as measures are debated.

An unfortunate reality of politics is the old saying "it's not what you know, it's who you know" rings true most of the time. Fortunately, in a short time, you can build your network simply by showing up and getting involved in clubs and campaign efforts. This can even lay the groundwork for an eventual run for office, if you are so inclined in the future.

Many elected officials began their service this way. In an interview with Chamber Business News, Congresswoman Debbie Lesko (R - Arizona) described how simply reaching out and showing up got her quickly plugged into the political process:

> *I was at a time in my life when I wanted to know who these people on the ballot are. I'm a Republican, so I called the state Republican Party and asked them if they had meetings and sure enough every legislative district in the state of Arizona has monthly meetings and I started showing up. There was Jan Brewer who was I think a county supervisor at the time and I just showed up each and every month.*

> *Before you know it, I was registering voters and getting really involved. I was this huge volunteer and then I got elected as the district Republican chairman, then an officer of the Maricopa County Republican Party, then an officer of the state Republican Party, and then an opening came up in the state House of Representatives. People said, "you should run Debbie," and I asked my husband what he thought. He said, "Why not? You volunteer all the time anyway."*

> *So, there I was, I ran. I won. I served six years in the Arizona House of Representatives, three years in the Arizona Senate and I was all set to run for senate president until last December when Trent Franks unexpectedly resigned. I took about a week and a half to decide if I wanted to run for U.S. Congress and I'm sure glad I did because here I am and plan to win again in November and serve another two years.[58]*

Because she showed up and volunteered her time, Congresswoman Lesko quickly moved up the ladder and began influencing the political process becoming a state representative, state senator, and eventually a congresswoman.

Jaded by political parties, but still want to be involved? There are places for you to serve outside of the establishment too. That is how State Senator Patricia Rucker (R - West Virginia) got involved.

> *I didn't like the direction the country was heading in. I can tell you; I was furious when George Bush did the bailouts. I just thought that is absolutely not the role of government. You have to let things fail.*

> *The whole point of opportunity is that you have the ability to succeed beyond your wildest imaginations, but that also means you have the potential to fail. But that sparked my interest and I thought 'oh no, this is not a good direction to be going.'*

Senator Rucker described how the Wall Street bailouts served as the catalyst that encouraged her to start a local Tea (Taxed Enough Already) Party in her community. When over two hundred people showed up to their first rally and her regular meetings frequently surpassed fifty attendees, she knew she had struck a chord and was not alone in her viewpoints.

> *When we first started my Tea party in my county, we had mostly Democrats running. There weren't even Republican options in most places on the ballot. I remember how disappointed I was to finally have the right to vote in America after becoming a citizen, but my ballot was blank. I didn't really have a choice. I just wanted to fill that in with some options, and very soon after the Tea party started, we started winning elections. By 2012, Republicans started winning the elections in Jefferson County.*

As an immigrant from Venezuela, she has seen firsthand how progressive policies can change a country for the worse and is determined to make sure the same thing doesn't happen to America. She didn't allow disillusionment with the Republican Party stop her from making a difference.

> *They [political establishments] take advantage of the fact that we're busy. It's no secret that most state legislatures and government bodies meet during the day when everyone is busy. Don't let them take advantage. Show up, get involved. You can join organizations that keep you abreast of what's going on, and then you can be the person who calls or emails your legislators to urge them to vote one way or another and influence your friends to do the same thing.*

> *When I first started the Tea party organization, I took all five of my children with me. But, guess what, it was a great education for them. All five of my children know how bills are made, they know how people get elected, they understand what is happening. So, don't feel like you can't participate because you have children. It was a great experience for them.*

Getting involved isn't difficult. It doesn't require running for public office; it simply involves showing up to a couple of meetings a month and volunteering your time and talents with your local Republican party, political club, or even a campaign.

With the rise of social media and "woke" outrage culture, it may seem on the surface that political activism has reached a highwater mark in recent years. However, how many people do you know who post angry social media rants are actually engaged and taking action?

Very few. If you simply show up, you will be welcomed with open arms. If you demonstrate your passion, it won't be long before you are given responsibilities, board positions, and other opportunities to become a political influencer within your community.

Clubs and Organizations

Depending on where your passions lie, you can join a variety of clubs and organizations in your local community. Some are more political than others, and some are more partisan than others. Some are affiliated with a national brand and some are organic and local, like the Tea Party movement.

If you are looking for something political, most communities have, at minimum, a Republican Women's club. Most of these clubs are affiliated with the state and National Federation of Republican Women.

The National Federation of Republican Women was founded in 1938 and describes itself this way:

"We empower women from all backgrounds in the political process and provide a forum for women to serve as leaders in the political, government, and civic arenas. Our objectives are to: Inform the public through political and legislative education, training and activity; recruit, train and elect Republican candidates; protect the integrity of our electoral process; promote the principles, objectives and policies of the Republican Party; unite and facilitate cooperation among the state and club organizations; and, increase the effectiveness of women in the cause of good government."

Republican Women clubs tend to meet monthly over lunch or dinner to hear from a speaker and discuss things they can do to encourage their local community to vote Republican. Some of these clubs even have Political Action Committees where they raise money to support local candidates.

The Texas Federation of Republican Women has semi-annual conventions where chapters from across the state gather to discuss their officers, legislative priorities, campaign activities, and hear from elected officials.

Joining your local Republican Women club could be a good starting point for you to meet some like-minded women, grow acquainted with your elected representatives, and become more comfortable with the political process.

Disillusioned with the Republican Party, but still conservative and want to be involved? Maybe it is time to join an organization that works on issues you care about. Whether it is supporting the free market, advocating on pro-life issues, reforming education, or working to reduce the size and scope of government, there is an organization out there that works on issues that matter to you.

Additionally, there are dozens of other quasi-political organizations you can join in your local community ranging from pachyderm clubs to Lions Clubs to Rotary Clubs.

One of the best ways to become informed, overcome the confidence gap, and build community is to join a Policy Circle. The Policy Circle is an organization made up of "a group of women who, like you, are concerned about their communities and want: 1) Discussions, not arguments, 2) Policy, not politics, 3) Facts, not feelings, and 4) More creativity, less red tape."[59]

The Policy Circle created a framework for women all across the country to talk about public policy in small groups. Similar to a book club, Policy Circles meet in someone's home or another comfortable setting to talk about policy in a roundtable discussion format. No pressure to perform, no judgment! Pre-prepared reading materials on topics such as the economy, education, health care, foreign policy, and immigration are provided ahead of time so that attendees can come better prepared to understand pressing issues and share their point of view. The format facilitates a deep, respectful conversation that helps everyone participating have a better grasp of the issues and see a range of perspectives. By creating an interesting and fun environment, these groups are helping women to be informed and invested in impacting public policy.

Ultimately, groups and conversations like this can help to bridge the imaginary gap that many women have created in their minds, helping them feel more confident and qualified to step into the public policy arena. Check out the ThePolicyCircle.org to learn more and find opportunities to get connected to an existing policy circle or start your own.

Other organizations to consider that cover a broad range of topics might include state think tanks, Heritage Foundation, Institute for Justice, Cato Institute, and American Enterprise Institute, just to name a few. Many of these, like the Texas Public Policy Foundation, also have groups specifically for young professionals.

Appointments

One often overlooked but influential way to get involved is to be appointed to a board or commission. While we have all heard of the high-profile federal appointments and cabinet positions, cities, counties, and states also have a broad range of appointed offices.

At the local level, there are opportunities to serve on various boards handling issues that range from planning and zoning to transportation to the arts. At the state level, there are commissions that regulate specific industries (such as the real estate commission or the board of dental examiners), commissions that carry out legislative directives (such as the education agency or health and human services agency), and task forces that make policy recommendations on certain topics (such as a criminal justice reform task force).

There are likely dozens of appointments that need to be made by your local city council member or county commissioner. This number can be in the thousands at the state level. For example, the Governor of Texas will make about 1,500 appointments during a four-year term.[60]

The elected officials making these appointments are always looking for good people to serve!

One important thing to note is that you do not have to be an expert in the area of jurisdiction to fill the role effectively. In fact, many industry specific roles require that they have members that are not a part of that profession. For example, the dental board may require that a certain number of seats are filled by members who are *not* dentists. This is important in order to bring a consumer perspective to the decisions that are made.

> Local and state elected officials are tasked with making appointments to many boards and commissions.
> They are always looking for good people to serve!

I learned the value of this outside perspective while serving at the city. If you fill an aquatics task force with pool enthusiasts, you will find that their recommendation is to spend all of the city's money allocated to parks on building more pools. In order to have a balanced discussion and have policy recommendations that are reflective of the community, you must have other impacted parties represented.

The time commitment for these positions is often very manageable. Some may meet monthly while others may meet quarterly or even semi-annually.

In order to be considered for an appointment, you likely only need to fill out a short application. Take a look at the boards and commissions that exist in your community and state and apply!

Becoming a Delegate

Want a hand in choosing the next President of the United States? Maybe you should be a delegate to the next Republican National Convention!

At the Republican National Convention, 2,472 representatives from across the United States gather to select the GOP presidential candidate. The eventual nominee will need the support of a majority of those delegates, earning at least 1,237 votes.[61]

Rep. Julie Emerson's first foray into politics was becoming a delegate:

> *I was in college when the Affordable Care Act was going through Congress. My intention was to go to medical school, so this issue made me realize I should start paying attention to politics and what was going on in the government.*
>
> *Around the same time, a friend of mine was a delegate to the Republican National Convention. I knew what it was generally – that the Convention was where the Presidential candidate for the party was nominated – but I honestly didn't really understand what happened there. I had a lot of questions. How do you become a delegate? What does it mean to be a delegate? I had no idea, but I went and met a lot of people and my interest grew.*
>
> *I ended up getting involved in some community events after I came home. One of the first political meetings I attended was the Parish Executive Committee – which would be the County Executive Committee for most people. While it was comprised of a bunch of men who were about three times my age, I was welcomed with open arms. Some of*

them I knew from church growing up and they exclaimed, "Little Julie! Good to see you here!" From there, I started volunteering on campaigns.

Similarly, Colorado State Representative-turned-County Commissioner Libby Szabo got her first exposure to politics watching her mother's involvement with the delegate process.

When I was a little girl, my mother was very involved in local politics. When she attended her caucus in Colorado, she would always drag me along. When I was younger, I would sit in the corner and color, but as I got older, I better understood what she was doing there. Seeing her involved instilled in me the importance of speaking up to improve our communities.

When I turned 18 and started voting, I started participating myself, eventually becoming a delegate to the state convention. I quickly realized that my one voice was representing about 5,000 people (the size of a precinct in her community) through the process. Being a delegate meant I was elected by my peers who supported and instilled confidence in me.

I dabbled and volunteered party politics for twenty years and had four kids during that time. It was great, because it allowed me to contribute and do something I was passionate about, while only having to commit a few months of my time every two years during the election cycle. I talked to voters door-to-door on behalf of the party and certain candidates, attended meetings to help shape our platform, and enjoyed being behind the scenes. The rest of the time, I was able to focus on raising my kids and running our family business.

The process for becoming a national delegate varies from state-to-state. In some states, delegates are elected directly during the primary, in other states delegates are elected at their local and state conventions, about a dozen states allow for campaigns choose their delegates, and still others are elected or appointed by their state party executive committee.

If you are interested in becoming a delegate, find out what your state's requirements are ahead of the primary and reach out to your local party chairperson to ask their advice on what you can do to get involved and earn a spot.

Volunteering on Campaigns

For many people, their first foray into politics involves supporting and volunteering for a candidate they believe in.

For conservative pundit, Laura Ingraham, Ronald Reagan's 1980 campaign for president served as a catalyst for her involvement to this day:

> *My best memory of when it really seemed solid, most solid in my mind, was when I was in high school during the election - I think it was ninth grade, and the election of Ronald Reagan in 1980. The college cafeteria - the high school cafeteria, Glastonbury High School, it was - we had an election night party, and there were all these tables for Jimmy Carter.*
>
> *There were, I think, two tables out of - and we had a big class, 430 in my class, there were two tables for Reagan. And the best as I can recall, it was a bunch of math geeks and then it was me and a couple of other people.*
>
> *And I'll never forget watching the returns come in, and a number of the teachers were really bummed out, and I*

remember getting on the table and just going, yes! Like I just pumped my fists and go, yes!

And Reagan really spoke to me at that age. And I think that this city, Washington, is filled with people my age, now 40 and above, who, they wouldn't be here if it weren't for Reagan. He really changed the political landscape and gave us all a sense that, wow, we don't have to feel bad that we're Americans.[62]

While in the long term it is probably better to put your faith in ideas, not people, for many it takes an inspiring personality to spark the ember in their heart for liberty. Sometimes a special person comes along and phrases things in just the right way to inspire you to get involved.

Campaigns cannot function without volunteers, and there are a variety of ways to offer this critical support. Consider volunteering for a candidate you like or a cause you care about. Your time and efforts will be greatly appreciated!

Campaigns cannot function without volunteers, and there are a variety of ways to offer this critical support. Consider volunteering for a candidate you like or a cause you care about. Your time and efforts will be greatly appreciated!

To get involved, all you have to do is reach out to someone running for office, and their campaign will quickly put you to work knocking on doors, making phone calls, or attending community events handing out literature. Uncomfortable talking to people? Campaigns can always use help with data entry and organizing information.

The campaign you volunteer for doesn't have to be something as high-profile as president or congress — it could be the campaign of a friend or neighbor who has decided to take on the challenge of running for school board or another local office.

Regardless if you decide to volunteer on a campaign, get involved with the Republican Party, become a policy activist, or network with a local club or organization, you will gain valuable exposure and knowledge of the political process.

If you are not able to contribute your time to a candidate or a cause, consider making a financial contribution. Campaigns are expensive to run. From purchasing voter lists, campaign software, and media ads to paying a campaign manager, consultant, and vendors, to printing literature, campaign signs, and t-shirts, everything has to be paid for by money the candidate works hard to raise. The decisions our elected officials make have a huge impact on our families and our pocketbooks. It is well worth the investment to donate to those who are fighting to protect your values.

KEY INSIGHTS

- Elected officials care about what their constituents think — they are the voters who will decide whether or not they serve another term.
- Very few people know who represents them at different levels of government. Find out, and then contact them to introduce yourself and discuss issues that are important to you.
- Local political clubs and civic organizations are a great place to become more informed and get involved.
- There are many board and commission positions appointed by your local and state leaders. Serving in this capacity is a great way to have an impact.
- Volunteers are absolutely critical to a successful campaign. Consider being one! If you can't give your time, give your money.

CALL TO ACTION

Contact the elected officials who represent you. Schedule a meeting with your school board or city council member, as well as your state representative and senator. Then, sign up to volunteer for the campaign of a candidate you support. You could be the difference in helping them to get elected!

7

How to Run for Office

You have already heard my story about how I decided to run for office. And by now you know, I am very supportive of the idea of you running for office.

While it is true there is never going to be a perfect time to run, that doesn't mean that there isn't a strategy to determining what to run for and when to run. A lot of thought and planning goes into a successful campaign. Be smart about what you run for, wait for an opportunity to step up, and strike as soon as that opportunity presents itself!

Sometimes it will be obvious: a long-term incumbent retires, and no one with your values steps up to run or your local Republican Party approaches you about challenging a vulnerable Democrat. Other times, you create your own opportunity: the incumbent has started voting in ways you disagree with, or, as in my case, the district boundaries are redrawn in a way that provides an opening.

Former New Mexico State Representative Yvette Herrell had this to say when we spoke about running for public office:

> There's no better way to influence your elected leaders than by being one. And there are so many ways to serve. While Congress commands a lot of the media attention, it's the state and local races that truly shape the direction of our communities.
>
> You don't need to raise a lot of money or have name recognition to run for something like your school board or city

council. Depending on the size of your city, your school board and city council may be part-time positions that meet in the evenings only a couple of times a month. If you're in a larger city, a council position often pays a salary that helps to compensate you for your time.

We often don't think about serving in this capacity unless a provoking event spurs you to action. But conservative women are woefully underrepresented in these offices and we desperately need common-sense leaders to step up and serve.

I couldn't agree more. Don't wait for something in the news to make you mad. Step up now and be a part of the solution before something spurs you into action. That way, when your action is needed, you are already in a position to make a difference immediately.

> "There's no better way to influence your elected officials than by being one!"

Deciding to run for office wasn't something Louisiana State Representative Julie Emerson took lightly. Like me, she spent months trying to find a qualified candidate to challenge the Democrat incumbent who represented the district she grew up in. Eventually, she determined it was time to step up and take the race into her own hands:

In 2014, my home state house district was represented by an individual who I felt was a little bit left of the values of my district. In our region, we still have a lot of so-called "blue dog democrats" who vote Republican but are still registered as Democrats. Sometimes they'll vote Democrat on the local level and then Republican on the national level. I felt like if someone got in there and worked really hard, that they could flip the district to red, because I knew the values of the area that I grew up in.

I decided to help find someone to run against him. For months, I talked with community activists and leaders, and the conclusion I heard repeatedly was that yes, the district could be flipped, but not until the incumbent decides not to run again. He was well-funded, young, dynamic, and well-spoken. He had a lot of energy and no one really believed that he could lose.

After a couple of months, they started looking at me saying: 'You probably have the best shot. You know how to do this.' My business was just taking off, and I was focused on that. It wasn't great timing for me. Plus, I like doing things behind the scenes, not being out front. But God has a sense of humor, and here I am.

Julie saw the need and stepped up. She had a busy life and a thriving business, but she understood the importance of having a government that reflected the values of her local community. While the timing wasn't what she imagined, she knew that she couldn't expect someone else to do something she wasn't willing to do herself.

As is often the case, political service isn't your idea, but something you are called to do by others in your community. That was the case for former Colorado State Representative and current Jefferson County Commissioner, Libby Szabo. Libby was active in politics from a young age and continued to dabble as a volunteer as she raised a young family.

One day, the head of my state party came to me, and I thought he was going to ask me to run the party's opera-

tions for my county. But that's not what he did, he asked if I would run for State Senate.

I looked at him and said, 'Gosh, I'm so flattered, but no thank you. When you find a candidate, I'd be happy to help with their campaign.' He was shocked that I had said no, so he went back and rustled up a bunch of people to call me and try to talk me into it.

I had no idea why he would ask me. I didn't have a political science degree, or whatever I thought I needed to be qualified. But I was always involved in serving my community, working in Sunday school at my church, coaching youth soccer, and other capacities. He said, 'You're a perfect fit for your community. You are your community in everything you've done.'

What is funny is that even though I had all of this experience being involved in the party and managing campaigns, my first inclination was to still say no. I had never thought about running for office myself, and I was happy in what I was doing.

I spoke to my husband and thought through whether or not it was a good thing for our family. At that point, my kids were old enough to kind of understand what it would entail. So, we prayed about it and we came to the conclusion that maybe this was the right way to serve our community, and off we went.

Szabo had been around politics her entire life and active in helping political campaigns in her spare time for years, yet she for some reason still felt unqualified and was hesitant to run.

You might be reading this with similar thoughts, but I am here to tell you that you are qualified. The very fact that you have hesitations means you take the idea of serving in public office seriously enough to be a good leader.

I would be remiss to start this chapter without a word of caution. No matter when you decide to run, plenty of naysayers will chime in to tell you that it is impossible for you to win. Don't listen. Campaigns are about overcoming the odds and achieving something that seems impossible. As long as you follow a basic strategy for a winnable seat, victory is within reach if you have the right message and work ethic.

But what if I lose?

So what! Abraham Lincoln faced a series of defeats before he won the presidency. George W. Bush lost his first political campaign. Ronald Reagan lost two presidential elections before succeeding at taking the White House. Even women profiled in this book lost their first races before ultimately being elected. In fact, Commissioner Libby Szabo is one of them:

> So, I ran for state senate in 2008 in a swing district, and I had a million dollars spent against me of negative media . . . Ultimately, I lost by 1%.

> It was a learning experience. The head of my state party came back to me in February and said that I actually won the House district I lived in, but just came up a little short in the other parts of the Senate district. So, I asked to see the data, and the numbers looked promising. Maybe this is what we were supposed to do.

> This time, I won. Off I went to the state legislature and all I wanted to do was to make a difference there. Even though I didn't win the Senate seat, it prepared me to more

effectively to run for the House seat. I see too many candi-
dates who try one time and they give up.

Losing a campaign isn't failure on your part but giving up is. As the classic adage goes, if at first you don't succeed, try and try again. Don't let a fear of failure hold you back from helping us taking back our country. Many candidates who lose their first election go on to win a subsequent one.

Do Your Homework

Before you make a final decision to run, it is important to do your homework and determine the right place to serve.

If you are a Republican and a Democrat won your congressional district with 67% of the vote, maybe you are better off running for your local school board seat that was won by a liberal with a 52% margin.

Flipping a seat to a different party is not impossible, but it doesn't happen overnight. Consultants and donors know this, so if you run for the congressional seat described above, you will have a much harder time raising money and finding volunteers, making your uphill climb even more difficult.

If you are able to win that local school board seat, you will be able to gain invaluable experience in both campaigns and political service and start to build a network that you can take with you when you run for higher office.

Encourage others who you support to run for and win these local positions within this congressional district, over time you can shift the odds in your favor from the ground up. You will also be building an army of policymakers and influencers who can make a positive change in your local community.

If you live in a Republican district, the game changes entirely. Is there an incumbent in the seat? Have they effectively represented your values? Are they responsive to their constituents? Are they well known and popular in the community? How much money do they have in their campaign war chest?

If the incumbent is flush with cash but voted to raise your taxes or voted against legislation that was important to you, maybe it is time for you to step up and challenge him. If you feel underrepresented, it is likely that others feel the same way and will support your efforts.

Once you have examined all of the available seats and the players involved, it is time to look inside yourself to figure out where your interests align with opportunity. Only you can make this decision, but this is also a good opportunity to talk with friends and family and get their thoughts.

Running for office and serving as an elected official is truly a family affair. If you don't have buy-in from your loved ones, you are less likely to be successful.

> Running for office and serving as an elected official is truly a family affair. If you don't have buy-in from your loved ones, you are less likely to be successful.

It is a huge commitment. During the campaign, I spent my nights making phone calls and my weekends knocking on doors. While in office, I sat through countless Council meetings that lasted more than 12 hours and had all kinds of community commitments.

I wouldn't have been able to do it without Caleb, who was my biggest supporter every step of the way. He was emotional support when I was up against seemingly impossible odds, and he was practical support when he was on dad duty on nights and weekends. I can't imagine how difficult it would have been without his unwavering commitment. This is true for most anyone serving in public office.

Once you have spoken with your family members and gotten them on board with your running, make sure you are aware of the election date and the various requirements and deadlines along the way. The requirements vary from community to community, state-to-state. Spend some time researching this, so you don't miss out on the opportunity to run. There is always some basic filing to do to get your name on a ballot, and often requirements for campaign finance reporting. Before you do anything else, familiarize yourself with these rules and make sure you comply with them prior to your campaign launch.

Launching a Campaign

So, you have done your research, figured out what you want to run for, and the timing is right - now what?

It is time to prepare to formally launch your campaign.

If you are able to afford a political consultant or campaign staff, they will likely help you with this step and have more specific advice. However, many candidates do not have these resources when they first announce and get started alone or with a small group of supporters and volunteers.

Unless you are running due to a sudden retirement or resignation, you should have at least a few weeks to plan out your formal launch. During this time, it is crucial that you act quickly and efficiently to ensure you have all of your ducks in a row.

The first thing you need to do is to put pen to paper, or fingers to keyboard as the case may be. A couple of things you will need immediately are a one-page bio of yourself along with three to five key issues you are going to focus on. These issues might clarify over time as you talk to people in your district, but it is important to find a consistent message and stick with it.

You should also take some time and create a list of people you think could be helpful on the campaign. These could be supporters you think would volunteer and help you knock on doors, prominent people within your community you think would endorse you and introduce you to their friends and neighbors, or friends and contacts who might be able to contribute or help you raise seed money to launch your campaign.

From there, schedule a photoshoot with a photographer to get both headshots and family photos. You will need quality photos throughout the campaign for your website, social media, push card (campaign literature), and advertisements. Get a variety of candid and formal photos, and make sure some of them are patriotic. If you have pets, don't forget to include them - voters love dogs!

Next it is time to find someone to make you a website and a logo. It doesn't need to be anything fancy, but it should look professional, so people take you seriously, and be sure to include a place to receive online contributions. Typical staples of campaign websites include pages with your bio, key issues, links to social media accounts, and a place to list news and endorsements.

Now it is time to do a little database building. Many email services offer free plans, so I recommend creating an account to house your contacts, which allows you to send out information to supporters, solicit contributions, and send press releases to the media.

You know more people than you think. Go through your email accounts and address books and pull as many as you can to start. Then go online and figure out the email addresses for your local newspaper and television reporters, talk radio and morning show hosts, and even prominent local blogs to create a media list.

As you get closer to making your announcement, it is time to create accounts on the various social media platforms you plan to use for outreach. At a minimum, be sure to create a Facebook page and a Twitter account. While Twitter won't impact much on the ground, it is a good way to keep the press and political insiders aware of campaign victories and show off how hard you are working. If you plan to do paid advertising on Facebook, it is important to research the latest authorization requirements, as approval can sometimes take weeks to complete.

When you are ready to make your formal announcement, put together a press release that includes some information about your background, ideology, key issues, and family. Don't forget to include a few quality pictures, as publications often use whatever images are easiest for them to obtain, and it is likely that the pictures used during the launch of your campaign will follow you for years to come.

I recommend launching your campaign during the week - between Tuesday and Thursday to get the most coverage. Try to send out your press release before noon to ensure you make the evening news and the next day's paper. Be sure to share the news on social media and with your email list. Don't forget to tweet a link to the press release!

The Early Months

Congratulations, you are now a candidate for public office!

How do you feel? Excited? Nervous? Ready to put the pedal to the metal?

What is your first inclination? Come out swinging? Put out a press release about the incumbent's shortcomings? Throw a massive rally to gin up support?

Pause.

These are all things you may need to do throughout the course of the campaign, but right now you are months away, and come Election Day, no one will remember what you are doing now.

So, what should you be doing?

Raising money, knocking doors, soliciting endorsements, and attending community events.

Sound too basic? Well, what do all good sports teams have in common? They are great in the basic fundamentals. This is no different than knocking doors and dialing for dollars.

Come thirty days out from Election Day, you will be glad you have saved your money and ammunition for when the voters are paying close attention. Trust me.

Raising money can be awkward, uncomfortable, and difficult to do, especially when you are a first-time candidate. While it gets a little easier when you are an incumbent, it is likely never something you will enjoy doing, but it is a necessary part of running for public office. Here is what Louisiana State Rep. Julie Emerson had to say about launching her campaign and fundraising:

I decided to get in the race in January of 2015. We knocked on every single door in the district, worked really hard to raise money.

People always ask me if my family was involved in politics and if they gave me a lot of money to run. I think they gave me maybe $200! And, God bless them for it! I was happy to get it, and of course they invested a lot more in me over the course of my life. But my campaign wasn't funded by my parents.

It's hard, but you basically have to call in every single favor with everyone you know. The first $40k or $50k that I raised was mostly from people who thought it was cute that I was running for office. 'That's adorable, poor thing! I'll just send her some money because I feel bad for her.' Pity money! But that was okay, I'll take it!

A lot of the traditional donors who commonly gave to Republican candidates didn't give me the time of day at first. They told me to go raise $40k myself and then come back with a plan and we'll talk. I'm sure I was really over- whelmed and freaked out, but what I remember is that I *thought, 'Okay! Let's go do this!' Maybe this is one of the advantages to running for office when you're young. You think you can do anything!*

Every good consultant will tell you, just sit down and write a list of 20 people you know who will give you $1,000. I didn't even know 20 people who would do that, but I started a list of people who I thought might give me money, and I started calling them and emailing them. Somehow, we got to $40k. Once we got past that hump, it started trickling in. I started getting endorsements from other elected officials and organizations. We spent about $150,000. It was a true grassroots campaign, and we won 51% to 49%.

In my race, our local election rules limit campaign contributions to $350 per person, an unusually low threshold as far as campaigns go. That means once someone donates $350 that cycle, they can't donate again. So, I took a different tactic - one of assuring people that I would not bother them again if they went ahead and contributed $350 now.

Every little bit counts. It's important to ask everyone to chip in, even if it's only $25. Having lots of small contributions adds up, and it demonstrates the breadth of your support.

Raising money is not fun, but it is a necessary evil that comes along with running for public office. Don't neglect this piece of the campaign just because it is difficult, awkward, and discouraging. You will be glad you have built up a war chest when you are thirty days out from Election Day and have money to advertise and send out direct mail.

For me, knocking on doors was always more fun than raising money. I truly enjoyed meeting my neighbors and hearing their thoughts and concerns about their local government. There is no better way to prepare for being an elected official than by hearing from the constituents you hope to represent.

Volunteers and fundraising are critical components of running for office, but unless the candidate is the most dedicated person on the campaign, you will not be successful. I saw this illustrated firsthand through the tireless work of my former boss, Representative Jason Isaac. He was the type of person who started block walking before the volunteers showed up and would continue long after everyone else was done for the day.

When he won his race for political office, he was also the underdog fighting against the liberal establishment that had controlled his district for eight years. Isaac didn't let this deter him from putting 100% of his effort into the race, and in the end, he not only flipped the seat to Republican control, but he won by an overwhelming majority.

Block walking, or door knocking by going door to door in an effort to educate voters about your campaign and earn their support, is one of the most effective ways to earn votes. And the candidate *must* be the hardest worker of all. Their effort sets the tone for the rest of the campaign volunteers and staff.

> Block walking, or door knocking by going door to door in an effort to educate voters about your campaign and earn their support, is one of the most effective ways to earn votes. And the candidate *must* be the hardest worker of all. Their effort sets the tone for the rest of the campaign volunteers and staff.

A word of caution: don't just start knocking on random doors. Purchase quality data and knock doors of your likely voters. This is especially important for primaries and local elections. Your local party leadership and local campaign consultant types should be able to steer you in the right direction for where to purchase the data. You can narrow down the people likely to show up based on their previous voter history and spend your most valuable resource, your time, connecting with those voters face to face.

Also, don't feel as though you must go through this endeavor on your own. Find a core group of passionate supporters or volunteers to knock doors with you. You can even recruit passionate students who are interested in politics and pay them a small stipend or hourly rate to help get the word out, which helps ensure you have a regular staple of door-knockers and allows them to make some spending money while gaining resume experience as they finish up school - a win/win.

Knocking doors is also an excellent opportunity to identify new volunteers and locations to place yard signs. I asked every person who said they were going to vote for me if I could put a campaign sign in their yard. Many said yes, and this was hugely helpful to building my name identification in my race.

Especially in local and down-ballot races, yard signs help build name recognition and create momentum for your candidacy. Doing something because everyone else is can work in your favor. Neighbors are more likely to support a candidate if they feel the rest of the community is doing so as well. Plus, nothing will get under your opponent's skin more than seeing your name plastered around the community.

One of the doors I knocked on early in the race opened to reveal a kind and curious man, whose name I came to find out was Tim. He was generally familiar with the city council race and had heard my name but wasn't sure where I stood on the issues. We had a short conversation on his porch when he called for his wife to come meet me. They invited me in to sit and talk more.

As a candidate, this is always a double-edged sword. Of course, you want to take the time necessary to educate them on your candidacy and earn their support, but at the same time, you have a list of

100 homes to get to that morning, and the clock is ticking. But it was hot, and a little break and some water sounded nice.

I accepted their invitation and we had a great discussion about why I was running (have I mentioned property taxes are out of control?) and the solutions I planned to propose if I was elected. After about 15 minutes, they asked for a yard sign and what else they could do to help.

Tim ended up being one of my most loyal supporters and best volunteers. He showed up many Saturdays to help spread the word. He stood at the polls during early voting. And like so many of the other volunteers whom I was so fortunate to have on my side, he took hours and days out of his personal schedule to get me elected. I am so grateful that I knocked on his door that day, and that I didn't pass up his offer to come inside.

It is not unusual for candidates to find support simply by knocking on a stranger's door and having a conversation. Former New Mexico Rep. Yvette Herrell described to me an experience of winning over a Democrat with kindness.

> When I knocked on the door, I knew their party affiliation (from my voter data list), and this person was not Republican. When he answered the door, it was an older gentleman, but his skin was beautiful. I noticed that he just had a beautiful complexion. Right away I gave him my spiel, and he was not very pleasant. "Why are you running? Why are you a Christian? What makes you believe in God?" Just really going out of his way to try to pick a fight.
>
> In my mind I thought he's not going to vote for me. I just need to get off the porch and move on. My district was actually 67% Republican, but I wanted those Democrat's votes too.

He could tell I never had held office, so he knew that knocking on doors was a new adventure for me. And I think he was just trying to use anything he could say to intimidate me.

The only thing I could get out of my mouth at that moment was: "What kind of moisturizer do you use? Your complexion is beautiful!" and you know what, the mood changed instantly. He actually said to me, "Neutrogena." He goes through the next five minutes, and he literally tells me his entire skin care routine. We actually had a really good visit; we didn't talk about politics anymore - we really did talk about Neutrogena.

I left, but here's the blessing. A couple of days later I'm still in that general neighborhood knocking on doors and this car pulled up to me as I was walking down the sidewalk. He rolled down the window and said "Hey! I voted for you!" And I said, "Hey, I bought some Neutrogena!"

I smile about that story because it made me realize that if we keep talking long enough with people, we will find the common ground.

Another good way of finding volunteers and gathering high-involvement supporters is to attend club meetings and events within your community. Some will be partisan (Republican Women Clubs, Tea Parties, etc.) and others will be nonpartisan (Lions Club, Rotary Club, HOA meetings, etc.). Sometimes you will be interacting with a large crowd (Fourth of July picnic, Memorial Day parade, etc.), other times you will be mingling with folks one-on-one or in small groups. Regardless, they are all great ways to find potential supporters.

As you work hard and become more comfortable with your role as a candidate, people will start offering you their endorsement. This helps you build momentum.

Interest groups such as Second Amendment supporters and right-to-life organizations often mail slates of supported candidates to registered voters ahead of Election Day. Many voters simply take these slates with them into the polling location on Election Day and check the box for all of the endorsed candidates. You don't need a bunch of endorsements to win, but they can be very useful in earning votes.

Home Stretch

You have now slugged through the early months, working your tail off knocking doors and raising money, and you are closing in on Election Day.

You have been conservative in your budgeting, and you have a decent sized nest egg to spend on political advertising leading up to Early Voting and Election Day. You have outmaneuvered your opponent and racked up endorsements from organizations and community leaders. You have built up an army of supporters to knock on doors and make phone calls. What now?

Now is the time to finish strong, utilize your hard-earned resources, and execute your game plan. Unleash everything you have left and call in every favor you can muster to give you every possible advantage going into Election Day.

If you can afford polling, it can be very helpful to you in determining which messages are resonating with voters in your district. Oftentimes the messages we think are most effective might not be. That is not to say you should change what you believe, but more so shift the focus of your messaging to things you believe that voters are also passionate about.

Additionally, your problem might not be what you are saying, but how you are saying it. Shoshana Weissmann is a social media professional at a think-tank in Washington D.C., and well-known Twitter influencer. Shoshana has battled a number of illnesses and had to frequently visit doctors as a result. In our discussion, she described how this led her to an epiphany about messaging:

> I remember if I told doctors certain things, like the way the pain felt, they wouldn't believe me. But, if I played it down a little bit, then I could kind of watch their reactions and see what they thought. I've taken that lesson into policy marketing - you kind of have to think about what people are going to be open to.
>
> What messages are just going to make people think 'oh no I'm not listening to this' or 'this is wrong,' and what kind of messages keep people's ears open. What messages will everyone agree with, including people of different parties and different backgrounds. Start with the stuff that's not controversial and figure your way out from there, so that the ears are still open, and you can get your message through.

Travis McCormick, a friend who has run several campaigns in Texas, expanded on this idea when we chatted about messaging and polling.

> A lot of candidates have gotten frustrated when I tell them not to talk about certain things or to phrase talking points in a specific way. When you are knocking hundreds of doors a week, it is difficult to hear that some of the things you are saying probably aren't resonating with voters. But at the end of the day, we have to allow for data to drive our talking points.

In races where we have really salacious opposition research on a candidate's opponent, candidates almost always want to go after their competition immediately, but that is not always the best course of action and is an excellent example of why we conduct polling.

There are a number of situations where you wouldn't want to attack your opponent at all. Say the poll comes back and you're winning significantly, and no one knows who your opponent is - why do you want to inform your voters of his existence, when he obviously hasn't. Say the poll comes back and the negative information you have on your opponent is ineffective or considered unbelievable by your target audience. You wouldn't want to hit them on that either, because it could lower your credibility with voters or stoke the fire and unleash his ammunition against you.

If you can afford polling, don't think you are smarter than the data - use it. There are a lot of campaigns that would love to have it.

As you inch closer to Early Voting, now is the time to start sending direct mail and buying airtime on TV, radio, and digital platforms. The key here is to stay consistent across all of your paid media. It may take your audience seeing the same message several times for it to sink in.

Far too often, candidates make the mistake of having each of their mail pieces contain completely unique looks and messages. I have had candidates call me asking why we are sending virtually the same mail piece today that we sent last week - thinking it was laziness on my part. But it's not, it's 100% intentional.

I get it. When you have to see the same mail piece repeatedly in its draft stage, you assume that the voters are as tired of the mail piece as you are. But that is likely not the case, and changing the look and messaging in your mailers is just going to confuse voters.

The odds are the voter simply glanced at the mail piece a few times before it went in the trash. The more consistent both the look and message of the direct mail is, the more likely the voter will remember and correlate that look and message with you when they vote.

Not all of your efforts during this time will be spent on paid media - there is a lot you can do to earn free publicity as well. You should also be working on getting opinion editorials placed in the paper by supporters about your campaign and calling in any favors you have with talk radio or morning show hosts to get some extra positive exposure.

Don't pump the breaks on knocking doors until the start of Early Voting. That is the point at which you will want to shift your manpower and resources into electioneering at polling locations. If you aren't running for president or governor, many people entering the polls will be undecided about your race. Having someone at the polling location holding up a sign or handing out literature could be the final push they need to check your name on their ballot. Even if you can't have a volunteer at every polling location, you can put up signs out front as one last reminder of your name.

Most of the early voting locations in my community happen to be inside grocery stores. This is great because it's convenient for people to stop by the voting booth on their way to pick up food for dinner. I, along with volunteers for my campaign, manned every polling location in the district for as many hours as possible while the polls were open.

Believe it or not, it's quite difficult to approach someone in a parking lot without them trying to hurry past or avoid eye contact. But I had worked really hard over the last several months, and I wasn't going to leave votes on the table now. I quickly figured out that a smile goes a long way, and people were generally willing to listen to a short talking point and take a pamphlet of information about my campaign as they were walking into the polls.

I could often tell whether or not I had earned their vote from this limited interaction. Some people would smile back and say "good luck!" while others would look away and keep walking. Many were undecided, and after reading my literature while in line to vote, would wave on their way out and say "I voted for you!"

People had seen my name on signs and mailers, but voters are always surprised and usually happy to meet the actual candidate in person. I'll never know how many votes I earned from talking to people in that parking lot, but I know it was enough to make it well worth it.

Election Day

Your alarm goes off and you jolt awake. You didn't sleep much last night anyway - too many thoughts racing through your mind. You begin second-guessing your choices and asking yourself if you could have done more.

You have worked hard and left it all on the field. Don't let the "what-ifs" plague your mind — you have a lot of work to do if you want to finish this race strong.

You start your morning by dialing into a couple of local radio shows, making one last plea to voters before you shower and head to a high-turnout polling location. You let the local television station know the polling location where you will be, so they can conduct one last interview with you as people start showing up to vote.

Then you spend the day weathering the elements trying to speak to every single voter entering the polling location. Your opponent is likely doing the same thing, and you have volunteers at all or most of the polling locations across the district.

As the polling locations close, you wrap up your electioneering and head home to get ready before the election night watch party. You're exhausted. The last thing in the world you want to do right now is converse and mingle with other people, but you do it anyway because a lot of supporters have invested time and money in your campaign.

The clock seems to move slower once the polls are closed. You are filled with anxiety as the early voting numbers are finally released. Good news, you are winning, but the race is tight. Supporters get noticeably more excited and confident that you will be successful.

Election Day results start to trickle in precinct by precinct, and you wish to yourself that the results would just come out all at once. You are up, you are down, you are back up again and you would give anything to just get off this roller coaster and rip the band-aid off. Meanwhile, you must continue to mingle and make small talk with the dozens of faithful volunteers who are just as nervous as you are.

Finally, around 10:00 pm, the final few precincts report and you have in fact won the race! Your phone rings - it is your opponent. The margin is too large for them to overcome, even with a recount, and they concede.

The local television reporters are all there, and the crowd waits for you to make a speech. You stumble through your prepared remarks but emphasize how thankful you are to everyone in the room and how excited you are to make a difference for your community in your new role.

You help clean up the venue and roll into bed around midnight. At first you can't sleep due to the excitement, but soon you drift off into the most restful sleep of your life. You did it. You stepped up and you were successful. And in a few short weeks, you begin the challenge of serving.

KEY INSIGHTS

- Don't wait, take action now. There's no better way to influence your elected officials than by being one!
- Look for the right opportunity, get organized, and make sure your family is on board.
- Focus on the fundamentals – block walking and fundraising.
- Follow a data-driven plan that ensures you're reaching the right voters and spending money on the right messages.
- Be the hardest working person on your campaign.

CALL TO ACTION

Run for office!

Campaign Checklist

Do your homework

- Examine the political landscape.
- Research the district and your potential opponents.
- Choose a position where your interests align with opportunity.
- Research state and local requirements, fees, and forms.
- Make sure your family is on board with you running.

Pre-Announcement

- Hire a seasoned campaign manager and/or a consultant (if you can afford it).
- Determine your platform and key issues.
- Create a list of potential donors, volunteers, and supporters.
- Hire a photographer to take high-quality headshots and family photos.
- Create a website and social media accounts.
- Create a database of contacts and media.
- Draft a press release and be strategic about the day and time of your formal launch.

Early Campaign

- Be the hardest worker on your team.
- Focus on fundamentals: raising money and knocking on doors using targeted voter lists.
- Recruit volunteers.
- Attend community events and candidate forums.
- Avoid attacking opponents. Save ammunition for closer to Election Day.
- Seek endorsements from issue advocacy groups and high-profile individuals.

Home Stretch

- Conduct polling to determine best messages for your electorate (if you can afford it).
- Have volunteers and signs at polling locations.
- Free Media: Appear on every talk radio program and morning show you can.
- Paid Media: Spend money on advertising (direct mail, radio, TV, online, etc.).
- Plan election night watch party.
- Spend time personally talking to voters outside the busiest polling location.
- Attend your election night watch party and, win or lose, celebrate your efforts.

8

How to Serve

Against the odds, you won a hard-fought campaign and will be sworn into office at the first of the year! Amazing! This is no small feat!

After you take an appropriate amount of time to celebrate, relax, and recalibrate, it is time to start the real work, getting ready to govern. You have a lot to do in a short amount of time if you want to hit the ground running immediately when you get the keys to your office.

Campaigning for office and actually governing are two very different things that require very different skill sets. Just because someone is skilled at communications and salesmanship does not always mean that they are good at public policy and statesmanship. Being a good campaigner also does not mean that someone is a good manager or has the tempered demeanor necessary to work with others and get things done.

On the campaign trail, you may have spoken generally about the need to eliminate property taxes and replace them with a consumption tax to fund government. You may passionately support this position, and truly want to make this happen while you are in office. However, if you fall on your sword and only accept 100% of what you want, you will likely be unable to bring any tax relief to your constituents. You may have to settle for a small decrease in the effective tax rate or even simply a limit on property tax growth to begin with.

On the campaign trail, you may have rolled out a plan to ensure every child in your community can attend the school of their choice. Again, you may be truly passionate about this plan and work tirelessly to get a meaningful proposal in front of your colleagues. However, the education establishment is a powerful force with lobbyists, money, and passionate employees to fight for their cause, so to get enough votes you may have to settle for a pilot program that gives vouchers to certain students with special needs.

If you are going to be effective in office, you have to realizethat the key difference between campaigning and serving is that you will never get 100% of what you want, 100% of the time. Campaigning is an all-or-nothing short game, with election day always looming at the end of the road. Governing is a long game, where it can take many years to chip away at the longstanding policies that you hope to change. The higher the office, the more this tends to be true.

Depending on the day, governing can be exhilarating and rewarding, or infuriating and draining. There is nothing like the happiness and relief that comes with finally passing an item that you've been

> Campaigning is an all-or-nothing short game, with election day always looming at the end of the road. Governing is a long game, where it can take many years to chip away at the longstanding policies that you hope to change.

working on for months, or even years, and knowing that your work has changed something for the better. On the other hand, there are days that you get thrown under the bus or a critical vote doesn't go your way or that an angry constituent's harsh words get under your skin. Serving in public office is truly a roller coaster of emotions.

To survive, you must keep your savior complex in check and realize that you are never going to be able to do everything for everyone. The serenity prayer is a great reminder that we can only do so much: "God grant me the serenity to accept the things I cannot change; the courage to change the things I can; and the wisdom to know the difference."

You Won! Now What?

Once you have won your election, you have a few crucial weeks or months to get your affairs in order to make sure you have everything ready when you are sworn in. It is good to be prepared so you can hit the ground running on issues important to your constituents.

This is also an important time to make sure you leave your campaign in a strong position in case you decide to run for reelection. This means being diligent about storing your data and coming up with a system of touching base with key supporters on a regular basis. It also means things as simple as collecting your yard signs and finding a place to store them until you are back on the ballot.

If the position you have won allows it, this is a great time to fundraise and start building a war chest for your next election. Post-election fundraisers are often successful because individuals who sat on the sidelines out of fear of selecting the wrong candidate will often donate money and help set you up for your next race.

Follow the news closely and try to become an expert on the key issues that will be coming before you when you take office. Be vigilant about continuing to visit with constituents about the issues that concern them. Keep records and a list of these concerns and try to find ways to address them as issues come before you.

If you were running against an incumbent or were the underdog in the race, it is likely that there are a lot of people who would like to make amends or establish a relationship. Unless someone was especially hostile to you or your family, I recommend you at least meet with them and hear them out. Who knows? In the next election cycle, they may be fierce supporters!

Simply being willing to hear from people, even those who disagree with you politically, is essential to properly representing your district. Much of what you will do as an elected official is apolitical - helping your constituents troubleshoot interactions with agencies and departments of government.

Former New Mexico State Rep. Yvette Herrell discussed this topic during our interview.

> *Not everything you do as a public servant, as a state representative, is about the bills and legislation. It's also very much about public service and being able to help connect people with those in agencies, like the Department of Veterans Services or Human Services Department.*
>
> *Just being able to make sure people are getting the service that they desire and need is important . . . I think that for me has been something I've appreciated being able to do. I enjoy being able to help people connect those dots to find solutions and then find closure.*
>
> *So much of the time that you spend is really in some ways, kind of customer service, helping constituents find solutions. I just appreciate that, I'm a problem solver. I've always been a little bit aggravated with state agencies that are slow to respond, because you know what, we are paying their salaries. These people work for, in my case, the state of New Mexico, so they work for the people of New Mexico.*

No matter how much you wish you could, you will never be able to solve every one of your constituents' problems with government help. You can do a lot to help the people of your district, but not every problem requires a government solution.

Congresswoman McMorris Rodgers discussed this when describing what she learned at the unity dinners she hosts in her Eastern Washington district.

It is just bringing 8-10 people together for dinner - very diverse people. We put our cell phones away and hear each other's stories, seeking to find unity, not uniformity. Unity in that we really want the best for each other and for our community.

At the beginning, these dinners were much more difficult than I anticipated. It wasn't just the difference of opinion on a particular issue; it was just how people viewed me as their representative in Congress. I walked away with this impression that they thought if I really cared, I could make their lives better by solving all their problems.

And people would share heartache and struggles and health issues and loss. People carried burdens, and I want to help. But I am fundamentally concerned that people are looking to the government to solve so many of these problems and thinking that, I, as their representative should be able to solve them. It's almost as if every societal problem is demanding a legislative solution, and that's not the case.

Many social problems are better handled by individuals, charities, and religious institutions, and most economic problems are better solved by the free market. Use your judgement in knowing when government intervention would truly help, and when it would only create additional regulation and red tape.

As you work through these issues, you will not

> Many social problems are better handled by individuals, charities, and religious institutions, and most economic problems are better solved by the free market. Use your judgement in knowing when government intervention would truly help, and when it would only create additional regulation and red tape.

be alone. You will have confidants and staff to guide you. This is why one of the most important things you will do in the months leading up to taking office is to find and hire loyal staff.

Sometimes, this is easy. You may have had a sharp campaign manager who is quick on her feet and has a deep understanding of public policy. Maybe the outgoing member was kind to you during your election and has a talented chief of staff who knows the district and wants to continue serving. Maybe you met someone over the course of the campaign who supports your platform and has experience working in government.

If that is the case, great - don't hesitate. Hire them before someone else does.

Sometimes, hiring staff is more difficult. If this is the case for you, take your time and really evaluate your options before you hire someone. Visit with other elected officials and see if they have any recommendations. Talk with a political consultant or the head of your local Republican Party and see if they know anyone who would be an asset.

What's important is staffing your office with people who believe in your priorities and will not undermine you behind the scenes. With so much information flowing in and out of your office, staff often act as a filter between the general public and the elected official. They are often the first people to see an email or hear a concern over the phone. They are the ones meticulously going through the day's news and sending you clips of what you need to be aware of to do your job. They are often doing the preliminary analysis on proposals and initiatives that come across your desk.

To be effective, you must surround yourself with people you trust, and your staff are a critical part of your success.

> To be effective, you must surround yourself with people you trust, and your staff are a critical part of your success.

Once you have your staff lined up, start thinking about what you will need to set up your physical office. Be sure not to let the swearing-in ceremony slip between the cracks — this is an excellent opportunity for you to touch base with supporters and invite them to take part and enjoy the fruits of their labors.

More than anything, as you prepare to serve, remember your campaign promises. You made a commitment to the men and women who checked your name on their ballot. You don't want to be another one of those go-along-to-get-along career politicians who you set out to defeat.

You also want to make sure that you remember who elected you. Former Rep. Yvette Herrell capitalized on this sentiment when she ran against a long-term incumbent:

> I think there was a hunger, an appetite, for maybe somebody younger, somebody with a little bit more energy, somebody who really was paying attention a little closer to the policy issues. It was a lot of work. I knocked on over 10,000 doors. It took me a year and a half to campaign, and it worked.
>
> But, I'm passionate about serving and for me it's always been and always will be people above politics. We see that so often where there are campaign promises made, but they are not always kept. I'm about relationships. I'm about building relationships with constituents.
>
> I'm not concerned about which party because I understand it takes everybody to come together to figure out ways that will find solutions. We have to find ways we can all work together in finding solutions that work for our future country, for our economy, for everything.

Remember your promises and those who supported you when you ran, and you can't go wrong.

Working with Others While Holding Strong in Your Convictions

Once you have been sworn into office, you will often be faced with conflict between maintaining your convictions and getting along with others in your elected body.

The key to governing effectively is establishing civil working relationships with all of your colleagues. Even if you disagree with someone politically, you can still be nice to one another, and you can always find common ground with one another on non-partisan issues.

Whether you like it or not, you build a certain rapport with the people with whom you serve. Your previous interactions build on one another, and your colleagues will quickly learn whether or not you are a person of your word. You spend a lot of time with one another, and you work on and think about the same issues (even if they are from different perspectives). More than anything, your colleagues are really the only people who truly understand what you are going through, because they are going through it with you.

I found an unlikely companion in City Council Member Ora Houston. She came out of retirement to run for city council at the age of 69 to represent her long-time community of East Austin, a majority-minority district. We voted in different political primaries for different parties, but she was kind and respectful. She also understood that many of the "progressive" policies being pushed by the council were hurting her constituents.

When the council wanted to pass a resolution mandating that every home have screens on their windows, she knew that this would be an added cost for many she represented who did not have extra money to spend. When the council passed an ordinance that required every new home to be equipped to install solar panels, she knew the estimated $1,500 additional cost would be passed down, driving the cost of housing up.

While we had different political perspectives, we found plenty of common ground. She is one of those rare people who is truly tolerant - listening when people talk and carefully considering what she hears. A survivor of domestic abuse, she stands up for herself with stately confidence that I admire. She does not put up with being pressured into political correctness or with anyone being treated disrespectfully, regardless of their views. She made those long nights in council chambers more tolerable.

Unfortunately, I wasn't as lucky with everyone else with whom I served.

I knew the left-leaning Austin City Council was not the place for a Republican to win on social issues, so I stuck mainly to the things I hoped to make real progress on in the fiscal arena. I found it more practical to work find common ground on topics that should be nonpartisan, such as taxes, accountability, and transparency, instead of picking fights I knew I would lose.

Unfortunately, that all changed the night Donald Trump became President of the United States. City hall became a much less tolerant and much more hostile environment overnight. Conservatives were now enemy number one, and while I was the same person I had always been, that included me.

I had worked with my colleagues for over two years by this point and was surprised that despite our history, some of them were unable to separate their hatred for Trump from their opinion of me. I had always passionately fought for my beliefs, but I did so in a reasonable, respectful way. Like other conservatives across the country, I was now collateral damage in the Left's culture war against anyone who did not share their fringe progressive beliefs.

To show their resistance to the new President, the Council began raising politically charged topics, despite the fact that they were not within our purview. In an effort to protest the border wall, they prohibited the city from doing business with companies that were working on border-related projects. To show their support for abortion, they provided free rent to Planned

Parenthood. While I had previously tried to steer clear of topics I knew were going to be unproductive, I was forced into the cross-hairs of the most heated and partisan debates.

After a crackdown on illegal immigration by the federal government, one council member capitalized on the opportunity to bring the immigration debate to city hall. He proposed a resolution that would re-allocate $200,000 of taxpayer funds to provide legal services for immigrants. A former community organizer, he rallied activists and summoned the media.

Regardless of your feelings about illegal immigration, this was not an appropriate use of taxpayer dollars. In a city that was rapidly increasing property taxes on residents, claiming not to have the funds necessary for basic city services, why were we spending money on something that was so clearly outside the scope of our responsibilities?

I knew this was going to be a day that tested my ability to stand my ground. I knew the item was going to be passed before it even came up for a vote. In fact, I knew I would be the only dissenting council member.

My staff recommended that I vote "no," but forgo making any specific statements about the item. That wasn't bad advice. With emotions running high, taking a stand on a politically charged issue like this would not prove to be productive with my colleagues. I only stood to damage the delicate relationships that I had, and potentially undermine my ability to work with them on other initiatives in the future. I didn't support this item for a variety of reasons, but I also knew this one would pass, and I needed to pick my battles.

While the council meeting convened inside, groups flying Mexican flags and chanting gathered just outside the chambers. I checked my emails from the dais, and one caught my eye.

It was from a constituent, and it said, "This isn't right. Please don't be a silent 'no' vote. Please speak up for us."

He was right. As difficult as it would be, I had a responsibility to speak up about why I didn't agree with this spending. If I didn't, there would be a footnote in every article that mentioned my dissenting vote, but no articulation of the reasoning why. The other side deserved to have a voice, and it was my responsibility to provide it regardless of how uncomfortable it might be.

As we worked our way through the agenda, I summoned my courage. When the item came up for a vote, I crafted my comments carefully and respectfully, saying something along the lines of, "Austin is becoming a place where the average family cannot afford to live, in large part because of the spending decisions that we are making at city hall. Those families who are struggling to get by should not be forced to pay for things like providing legal services to illegal immigrants. There are many non-profit organizations that provide these kinds of services. If this is a cause that is important to you, consider making a donation to one of these organizations. Put out a call today for people to voluntarily contribute to those groups."

The council sponsor spat back with something to the effect of, "You are a racist who is spreading deliberately misleading information and trying to score points at the expense of the vulnerable."

When he made the accusation that I was "racist," I was shocked. We normally tried to keep a certain level of civility on the dais, and this was clearly uncivil, as well as unfounded. His comments stung, but I knew that I could not let them go unchallenged. And, I was absolutely certain that I was not the person in this conversation who was trying to score political points. I tried to compose myself and worked unsuccessfully to keep my emotions in check in my response. I explained that the debate about illegal immigration is a valid one, but that the Austin City Council is not the legislative body with jurisdiction over the issue. I understood that he was unhappy with a federal policy, but I didn't think that gave him a right to spend other people's money just to send a token message.

After several tense exchanges, during which I was hissed at and booed from the audience, we took the vote. It was ten to one. I knew that my decision to raise a dissenting opinion on this heated topic would not be easy. But it had gone even worse than I expected.

Later that day, I found an email response in my inbox from the same constituent. It said, "Thank you for standing up for us."

The working relationship between that council member and myself was never the same. I had lost the vote and the camaraderie of that colleague, but I gained the trust and respect of a constituent, and that is what mattered. I was not elected to the city council to make friends; I was elected to stand up for the constituents I was blessed to represent.

Serving as an elected official is a constant test of the strength of your principles and resolve. Compromise is a tricky thing. On one hand it is essential to governing, especially if you are in the minority, as I was. On the other hand, you do not want to sell out your values or constituents.

To get a majority of your colleagues to support your initiative, you will have to compromise in some way. Where do you draw the line? When is it worth it to concede a little to get most of what you want? When has a policy gotten so watered down that it is no longer worth your support?

These are the questions you will constantly be faced with and only you can answer. I grappled with these questions almost every day during my time in office. There is perhaps no better example than when the city council decided to go after the ride-sharing market, essentially forcing Uber and Lyft out of Austin.

A Critical Vote

As the only conservative on the city's governing body, the Austin-American Statesman later chronicled my term with the headline, "To her supporters, she's Joan of Arc. To her council colleagues, she's undermining the city."

This headline encapsulates how many people - depending on their politics - viewed my service during the numerous battles I fought while on the city council. Perhaps the fight to keep ridesharing platforms like Uber and Lyft in Austin best explains this dichotomy.

Austin prides itself as a hip city, up to date on all of the latest trends and technology. Elected officials like to brag about all of the high-profile companies that have moved their headquarters or expanded their presence here.

Ridesharing and Austin seemed tailor-made for one another. With a bustling university, vibrant downtown, and limited parking options, Uber and Lyft quickly became a popular method of transportation when they entered the market.

Ridesharing or transportation network companies (TNCs) operate as an on-demand service from an application on your smartphone. The app allows regular people to make a living or earn additional spending money by using their own cars, during their own free time, to drive around other members of their community. The results have been incredible as TNCs have driven down costs for consumers, reduced instances of drunk driving, and created thousands of jobs that otherwise would not exist.

Uber was founded in 2009 and started the ridesharing trend. Shortly thereafter, Lyft emerged as Uber's major competitor.

Unsurprisingly, Austin was an early adopter of ridesharing services. Guidelines for operation were put in place by the previous city council in 2014, and TNCs became quite popular with residents - both those enjoying the convenience of the service and those earning income from driving.

I was a year into my city council term when a group of taxicab operators stormed city hall angry about the competition, complaining about an uneven playing field. For the next year, I was at the center of an intense fight between taxi companies and TNCs to determine the fate of for-hire transportation in Austin.

On one side, taxi companies argued that TNCs should have to operate under the same draconian rules they did, which would entail these apps basically becoming another cab service with a cap on the number of drivers, trip rates set by the city, and fingerprint background checks.

Uber and Lyft argued that they were filling a different need in the market, providing flexible, part-time jobs for drivers, and a better customer experience for riders, all through an innovative new platform that was incompatible with the outdated cab system that had remained relatively unchanged for nearly 100 years.

To complicate matters, many of my council colleagues, with an average age of over 55 years old, had never used a ridesharing service. They lacked the context and user experience to understand the differences between the two models. It had also probably been a while since they had been stuck on 6th Street in Austin's entertainment district, fighting with floods of intoxicated college students to find a cab ride home.

Uber's argument that the crux of its success was having enough drivers on the app to quickly fill consumer demand with low wait times fell on deaf ears. Lyft's contention that its thorough background checks on their drivers, combined with sharing driver's license plate data and real time GPS coordinates of the trip with their riders, helped to improve safety for everyone was not fully comprehended by policymakers who had never used the app.

Weighing in on the value of TNCs when it comes to safety, the city's chief of police said, "I think the worst thing that could happen would be to lose 10,000 options for our citizens at two o'clock in the morning. We have people that are being victimized in this city, because they don't have an opportunity to quickly get into an Uber or a taxi. The worst scenario would be to limit the opportunities for our people that are vulnerable, in a vulnerable state, vulnerable time of night to leave the area and get home."

I felt for the taxi-cab operators, to an extent. They were scared about their ability to compete and uncertain about the future of their business model. But there are two ways to level the playing field: you can deregulate the side with more barriers and provide it with more flexibility, or you can place additional regulations on the side with fewer barriers and make running a business more difficult. The taxi-cab companies were uninterested in reducing the regulations on themselves or adapting to changing market demands; they were only interested in raising regulations across the board to drive their competition out of the market. Protection-ism at its finest!

Unfortunately, they found a sympathetic audience in the Austin City Council, which proposed a sweeping ordinance that would drastically change the way ridesharing services could operate. Forbes described the proposed rules as an "extensive list of petty, burdensome, and unnecessary regulations."[63]

The fight was fierce. It consumed seemingly all of the Council's time and energy, with hearings that lasted into the wee hours of the morning. Ridesharing drivers rallied on the steps of city hall, while taxi drivers filled the council chambers. At one point, Uber launched a horse and buggy service named after the Councilwoman who was spearheading the changes, in an effort to illustrate the outdated measures being proposed.

Uber users who logged into the app were notified that they could choose to forgo the on-demand car service and instead opt for "Kitchen's Horse and Buggy." For a cost of $50, customers could summon the antiquated form of transportation, named after my colleague, Ann Kitchen, who was leading the charge against ridesharing.

This tactic did not go over well. The fight was now personal, and as a result, the arguments spun out of control. The council moved further away from facts and data and became caught up in passionate personal anecdotes and vendettas.

At one point, the mayor, Steve Adler, proposed a system designed to incentivize drivers to submit to a city-administered fingerprint background check, or rather, penalize those who did not do so. If a driver completed the city's process, they would earn the ability to display an additional badge on their cars and in their profiles. Drivers without this badge would be prohibited from picking up riders from the busiest parts of town, like areas near downtown nightlife, events, and festivals.

The TNCs saw this for what it was: the creation of a two-class system that added an extra layer of bureaucracy, unnecessarily complicating a system that was working well. Uber said this about the proposal:

> The mayor's badge proposal is a solution without a problem. It would effectively mandate duplicative background checks for drivers to access the busiest parts of the city where Austinites and visitors need a ride. Removing drivers' access to the airport, the entertainment district, and major events such as ACL and SXSW would cause increased congestion and limit transportation options where they are needed most. This is not about choices or incentives, but about protecting incumbent transportation providers. It's weird, even for Austin.[64]

Meanwhile, the threat of losing ridesharing services in Austin had ignited a citizen's petition that was headed for the ballot in the next election. If passed, the city would more or less revert to the original regulations that governed TNCs, nullifying the additional rules and keeping ridesharing services operating as they had before this fiasco began.

The controversy was making national and even international news and was becoming an embarrassment to Austin's reputation as a technological hub. The irony of a city hailed as the next Silicon Valley shutting down innovation that had literally transformed the way people thought about transportation was not escaping most people. It was a game of political chicken, where egos ruled the day, and thousands of riders and drivers were collateral damage.

The mayor was growing desperate to find a way to navigate the city out of this situation. He understood both the practical and political consequences of driving ridesharing services out of Austin (pun intended), but he also had to find a way to appease the majority of council members who were adamant about seeing their new regulations through.

On the eve of the critical vote, we were coming down to the wire. The Mayor had been working behind the scenes on a Memorandum of Understanding (MOU), trying to thread the needle between the two sides and save face for the city. The Austin-American Statesman reported:

> (The mayor) and his staff, meanwhile, have been feverishly working toward a compromise this week meant to avoid holding an election while somehow creating a situation where a sizeable number of ride-hailing drivers would agree voluntarily to undergo fingerprint-based background checks.

> That work extended deep into Thursday afternoon as (Mayor) Adler worked behind the scenes to craft a side agreement [MOU] that would accomplish that fingerprinting goal and somehow pass muster with Uber and Lyft and his council colleagues. The idea was that the council would adopt the petition ordinance, thus cancelling the election, and the side agreement.[65]

In addition to the two-tier driver system, which made certain areas of town off-limits for drivers unless they went through additional city-run screenings, the MOU included increased fees for ridesharing services to operate in the city, and mandatory reporting of confidential data to the city. It also implied a whole host of additional regulations for services that did not sign the agreement, such as fire extinguishers in every car and redundant vehicle checks.

I had been a holdout. A frequent user of Uber and Lyft, I saw the services as invaluable for a broad range of reasons. Most importantly, they helped to keep drunk drivers off the road late at night and provided reliable transportation for many people in a city where public transportation options are limited. Throughout the debate, I had been a fierce and outspoken advocate for ridesharing services and saw the efforts started by the taxi companies as nothing more than a way for them to use government to stamp out their competition.

And I wasn't alone. The council had been overwhelmed with testimonials about how ridesharing had changed lives and improved our community for the better - students, musicians, and newcomers who had been able to earn a paycheck on their schedule, disabled residents who had access to a reliable, on-demand way to get around the city, and commuters who had given up their cars now that they had an affordable way to get to work.

This issue did not come to the city council's attention because of constituent concern or outcry, but rather by competing business interests. The city's regulations were problematic because more than fifty percent of ridesharing drivers worked fewer than 10 hours per week, requiring these potential part-time employees to jump through redundant and unnecessary hoops makes them less likely to complete the hiring process. The new rules would reduce the number of drivers on the road available for hire, leading to longer wait times for customers and higher prices for rides, eventually causing a decrease in demand. In other words, it undermined the very things that make ridesharing successful — a fast, safe, reliable, high-quality service at a low cost.

Behind the scenes, the mayor was counting votes. The Council was split 5-5, and I was the swing vote. The mayor needed me to support the MOU for it to pass and to avoid a citywide referendum election. All other avenues of compromise had been exhausted. We had started the council meeting at 10:00 am, and twelve hours later, emotions were running high.

Both Uber and Lyft had given in and were reluctantly agreeing to comply with the new regulations outlined in the agreement.

I had a choice to make. I could vote "yes" and allow all parties to move on from this issue, please my colleagues, and prevent what was sure to be a divisive election on the issue. But this would require me to abandon the principles that had guided me so far throughout this debate - a belief that the free market was working, competition is good for consumers, and that we didn't need to "fix" something that wasn't broken by adding unnecessary regulations.

Or I could vote "no," sending the issue to a public vote and hope that the results of the election, or even the state legislature, would rectify the mess that had been created.

I had worn my favorite red blouse that day, hoping it would give me the confidence I needed to navigate my way through the high-stakes decision. We had taken a recess and the mayor had retreated to his office on the second floor while he worked on the negotiations. The clock was ticking, and the council members were due back to the chambers soon. My staff and I huddled behind the dais as I quietly but urgently updated them on the situation. I trusted them wholeheartedly and valued their opinion.

"Everyone else has agreed. He needs my vote," I said.

We talked through the options and tried to play each of them out. Was the MOU good enough to settle for? Are the sacrifices worth saving the city from what was sure to be a divisive public campaign? Would the mayor assist me in another initiative that would be worth trading support for? Will my colleagues ever talk to me again if I don't go along? We agreed on what needed to be done.

My phone rang. It was the mayor calling.

"But Uber and Lyft have signed off," the mayor begged, unable to understand what my hesitation was. I did not care what the companies had agreed to. The positions and votes I had taken were never about pleasing them, it was about doing the right thing for the city and the people who were depending on us.

Voting "no" wouldn't be easy, but it didn't feel right to vote "yes."

"I can't do it. My answer is no," I told him.

I was emotionally and physically drained. And, I was uncertain about what would happen from here. But the decision had been made, and without the votes to move forward, the agreement fell apart.

The fight was taken to the public arena, where purposefully confusing ballot language and a mishandled campaign led to a defeat that I did not believe accurately represented the will of the people. After all, more registered voters had signed the petition in support of TNCs than had voted against the proposition. Regardless, forced to comply with unworkable regulations, Uber and Lyft made good on their promise to leave the city, stopping services within days and disabling their apps in Austin.

The pain was felt immediately as drivers were left without work, and people who depended on the services were left with one less way around town. I received emails from business owners who changed their plans to relocate their operations to Austin, conference organizers who were moving upcoming events planned for our convention center, and tourists who were cancelling their plans to visit the city.

Was this my fault? Had I made the wrong decision that night in the Council chambers when I had the ability to avoid this altogether? Had I let my idea of "perfect" get in the way of achieving good? Should I have been more flexible in my principles?

I asked myself these questions countless times over the next weeks and months. But fortunately, the story wasn't over.

A few months after the city election on the ridesharing regulations, the state legislature convened in January of 2017. They had considered putting a statewide framework into place previously, and after Austin's debacle, the issue was resurrected. Different rules between neighboring cities and jurisdictions made regulations difficult to navigate, and the legislature had significant concerns about the impact this was having on the state's economy. It didn't hurt that it would be a political win for Republicans in the legislature to be able to step in and redirect the misguided actions of the liberal Austin City Council.

Legislation was filed and the state was set for another showdown - this time the venue was the state capitol, just a few blocks away from city hall.

In support of state licensing, Governor Greg Abbott said, *"Texas has for a long time been the home for innovation and economic growth, but a patchwork quilt of compliance complexities are forcing businesses out of the Lone Star State."*[66]

My input as a key figure in the Austin debate would carry a lot of weight. As the bills worked their way through the system, the Chairman of the Senate Committee on Business and Commerce called. The legislation had been set to be heard at an upcoming committee meeting, and he wanted me to testify.

The black market of ridesharing that had popped up in Austin in the void of more sophisticated companies was dangerous and scary. A Facebook group with almost 40,000 members connected anyone who wanted a ride with someone who is willing to give them one, without any affiliation with a ridesharing platform or background check. Hundreds of people had been stranded in the rain one busy night when one of the new local apps crashed. And, I worried about how drunk college students were getting home in the early morning hours.

My district had also voted in favor of the ultimately doomed proposition, and I knew I was defending what the majority of the people who I represented wanted.

Entering the capitol on the day of the hearing, I was relieved to be in a less hostile environment than city hall. I had spent many years working in this building, and I knew my way around.

After dealing with this issue for well over a year now, I knew it backward and forward. I had practiced my testimony and I was confident in my statements. My preparation paid off. My testimony was well-received, I responded to questions competently, and I handled the bevy of media interviews following my presentation with ease.

Ultimately, the Texas Legislature passed statewide regulations that closely resembled Austin's original ordinance and overrode the new regulations. Everyone in the state now played by the same rules – drivers were able to onboard quickly after passing a background check performed by the companies, the municipal fights being waged in certain cities ceased, and the free market was restored.

Uber and Lyft returned to Austin on May 29, 2017.

Had I gone against my principles and agreed to the MOU that night, chances are that the additional regulations in that agreement would have become state law. Taxi-cab companies and some cities would have argued in favor of them, and Uber and Lyft, who had signed off on the deal, wouldn't have had any leverage to argue otherwise. Who would have been left to fight for the drivers and consumers who benefitted from the less burdensome regulatory environment that led to better services and lower prices?

The impact of this policy decision spread far beyond Texas. A 2019 VOX article that chronicled the story highlighted the importance of the Texas law: *"It set a national precedent. There are now more than 40 similar statewide laws . . . making it easier for the companies to establish themselves all over the country and standardize their operations."*[67]

By sticking to my principles and playing the long game, I had made a difference not only in my community, but statewide and, perhaps nationwide as well. I had made the right decision.

KEY INSIGHTS

- Serving requires a different mindset from campaigning. Make amends with those who may not have supported you, and keep an open door to those who disagree with you.
- Hire sharp, loyal staff who will help you follow through on your campaign promises.
- Develop personal relationships with your colleagues. Even though you'll have disagreements on policy matters, it will be easier to pass initiatives that are important to you — and long meetings will be more tolerable — if you have a good rapport.
- Compromise is a reality of serving, but don't forgo your convictions. Where to draw the line is different for each issue and ultimately up to you.

CALL TO ACTION

Build a small group of trusted constituents and friends who will help you stay true to your values and beliefs. This will help keep you focused on the priorities that are most important to you and those who voted for you and prevent you from being pulled into a political bubble that can lead you astray.

Final Thoughts

Once you become an elected official, people start treating you differently, both professionally and socially. You have to learn whom to trust. (I'll give you a hint: it is almost always the same people you trusted BEFORE you got into office.)

Throughout my term, including the ridesharing debacle and so many other fights, it was a grueling process to stick to my principles in the face of heavy opposition. It was critical to have people whom I trusted on my staff and outside of city hall to serve as my sounding board and to keep me grounded. I had to develop a thick skin to shield myself from the biting words of those who disagreed with me.

More than anything, I constantly reminded myself that I represented more than just the organized groups and special interests in the echo chamber of city hall. The majority of the people I represented didn't have the time or ability to be at city hall for a twelve-hour long meeting in the middle of the workday or late into the evening. I represented people who couldn't take the time off work, who were busy picking kids up from school, and who were trying to get dinner on the table for their families. I represented the people I ran into at the grocery store, the people whose doors I knocked on while running for office, and the people who voted for me, trusting that I would do my best to represent the ideals that I espoused on the campaign trail.

It was these people I thought about when making the difficult decision whether or not to run for re-election. Conservative Austinites had very few voices standing up for them at the local level, even though Republicans made up about 35% of the city's population. I felt a crushing weight of responsibility on my shoulders, that I couldn't let these people down and leave them without a voice.

When the time came to consider re-election, I was pregnant with our second child and the thought of another four years of daily political commitments weighed heavily in my decision process. I knew that no matter what, I wanted to continue to be politically involved, but I wasn't sure that serving in my current capacity was the best way to be impactful.

Still, I felt a sense of responsibility to the constituents who put their faith in me. I went back and forth for months in my head as to whether or not I should run. One week, I was all in, ready to take on another four years. Other weeks, I would be discouraged and overwhelmed and wish I could pass the torch to someone who shared my values and had the name recognition and resources to win.

I earned a reputation as the "Voice of Reason." If I did not run for re-election, who would serve as that voice?

So, my husband and I prayed about it. The first time I ran for office it seemed so right. No matter how out of my element I was, it still felt like what I was supposed to be doing. I waited for that same feeling of confidence to come, but it never did. The longer I swayed back and forth, the more I wondered if this just wasn't in God's plan.

A friend of mine could sense how much this decision was weighing on my soul. One night at dinner, she said to me: "It's not your responsibility to carry the entire burden for all of us. Of course we want you to run again. But I don't see any of the people asking you to commit to another four years offering to step up and do it themselves. You're fighting a lonely battle, and we're so grateful for it. Instead of guilting you into serving another four years, we should be thanking you for the time that you have already put in and helping you find a suitable candidate to replace you. You have already sacrificed so much for us and for this city. There are so many other ways for you to make an impact if this doesn't feel right."

I cried, relieved that someone was giving me permission to make the decision that was best for my family at this moment and not carry the weight of the world on my shoulders. Shortly after, I made the difficult decision to not run for re-election, knowing that I would find other ways to be involved in my community.

I completed my four-year term in 2019 confident that I had been true to my word, voted my conscience, and represented my district to the best of my ability. I could hold my head high that I stepped up during my community's time of need and made a tangible difference.

Property taxes were lower than they would have been without my efforts, Austinites had access to ridesharing services, and the parks in my district were better off than when I arrived. I brought attention to and helped to eliminate wasteful spending and was able to increase transparency and accountability in several ways. I had served as the "Voice of Reason" and provided representation to a constituency in Austin that was otherwise overlooked and marginalized.

Since leaving office, we've added a third child to our family, and I've had the time necessary to grow my real estate business and provide for my family. In time, my friend proved to be right - there were plenty of other ways I could continue to serve my community outside of the city council.

I am now able to leverage the experience and institutional knowledge that I gained on the city council and as a legislative staffer in my capacity as a Senior Fellow at the Texas Public Policy Foundation. Through this role, I have been able to advocate for property tax reform at the Texas Legislature and play a role in passing landmark legislation that will lower taxes not just in Austin, but for people all across the state.

Leaving public office has also given me the time to focus on my passion for encouraging other conservative women to get involved in politics and run for public office. Through my podcast, Step Up, I have been able to share my story and the stories of other inspiring women with a whole new audience. I also reach thousands of listeners in Central Texas through my radio segment every week to inform them about what is going on in their government. And, I continue to have a platform to speak and write about the most pressing issues facing our state and country.

Maybe God's plan was for me to use my experience as a way to inspire others to serve. With strength in numbers, we can accomplish much more together than I ever could alone.

We can do better, but more of us need to get involved to make that happen. More women, like you, need to run for office. There is no perfect time to run, and it will require a tremendous sacrifice for your family and your pocketbook. But it is important.

If you are unable to run, you can still make a difference by getting involved. Whether it's volunteering for a candidate you believe in, joining an organization that is leading the charge on an issue that inspires you, or simply scheduling meetings with your elected officials to talk to them about what's important to you, your voice matters.

By running for office and stretching beyond what I thought were my limits, I have become the person I am today. And I'm endlessly grateful for it all.

This is my story, and the next one can be yours. All you have to do is STEP UP!

ACKNOWLEGEMENTS

This book, along with the advocacy that is chronicled here, would not have been possible without the unending support of my husband, Caleb. I am more grateful for and more in love with him every day. I wouldn't have this story to tell without the volunteers who dedicated their time and passion to my campaign - Dede Hebert, Judy Fox, Mary Beaver, Tim Moore, Andy Smith, and Peter Smith and many, many others. Travis McCormick helped me to tell my story in a way that captured my intentions to relate, encourage, and motivate. My staff, Michael Searle, Viveca Martinez, Brian Thornton, Catherine VanArnam, and Alice Claiborne, were in the trenches with me and gave me the willpower to continue the fight. Jason Isaac gave me the confidence to be bold, the opportunity to grow, and the encouragement to run. Phil King provided my first job in politics, igniting my passion for policy. My editors, Laurel Simmons and Paloma Ahmadi, helped to bring the book to completion. Elizabeth McCormick kept everything else on track so that I could devote my time to this project. The Texas Public Policy Foundation has provided a platform for continuing my advocacy and works to further the principles I believe in.

My parents, Susan and Rex Gale, lead by example, showing unconditional love and kindness to their children and those around them every single day. To my children, Juliette, Margaret, and Brooks, I hope I have made you proud. And last, but certainly not least, thank you to the many women who lent their stories to this book and the countless others who are leading in their families, communities, and governments every day.

Endnotes

Chapter 1

1   https://www.cawp.rutgers.edu/women-us-congress-2019
2   https://www.rollcall.com/news/politics/100-years-wom-en-congress
3   https://www.globalcitizen.org/en/content/she-should-run-250kby2030-campaign/

Chapter 2

4   https://www.merriam-webster.com/dictionary/feminism
5   https://www.courant.com/news/connecticut/hc-xpm-1999-03-27-9903270533-story.html
6   Source: https://web.archive.org/web/20170125034852/https://www.womensmarch.com/mission/
7   https://news.gallup.com/poll/235646/men-women-general-ly-hold-similar-abortion-attitudes.aspx
8   https://www.forbes.com/sites/carrielukas/2019/07/23/one-type-of-diversity-never-seems-to-matter/#67c76d1954da
9   https://www.nytimes.com/2018/10/06/opinion/lisa-murkow-ski-susan-collins-kavanaugh.html
10 https://www.theguardian.com/us-news/2016/feb/06/made-leine-albright-campaigns-for-hillary-clinton *https://en.wikipe-dia.org/wiki/Billy_Graham_rule*
11 https://twitter.com/robertfoster4ms/status/1148791254513258496?lang=en
12 https://denver.cbslocal.com/2019/04/30/handshakes-compa-nies-considering-banning-physical-contact-work/
13 https://www.washingtonpost.com/lifestyle/style/the-bil-ly-graham-rule-doesnt-honor-your-wife-it-demeans-her--and-all-women/2019/07/11/c1ac14e6-a380-11e9-bd56-eac6bb02d01d_story.html
14 https://www.wsj.com/articles/jim-mattis-duty-democracy-and-the-threat-of-tribalism-11566984601

15   https://www.cnn.com/2019/10/30/politics/obama-cancel-culture/index.html

16   https://www.linfield.edu/assets/files/admission/Visit/Events/CSD/LSVW19_IR_Reading.pdf

Chapter 3

17   https://www.cleanairact.org/news/documents/AAP-CA2019StATSReport-FINAL-April2019.pdf

18   https://cei.org/blog/how-much-will-green-new-deal-cost-your-family?gclid=EAIaIQobChMIvOi_x9235QIVgsDA-Ch13iAbxEAAYASAAEgJ3_PD_BwE

19   https://www.texaspolicy.com/battling-climate-change-does-not-empower-women-around-the-world-electricity-does/

20   https://www.npr.org/2019/09/23/763452863/transcript-greta-thunbergs-speech-at-the-u-n-climate-action-summit

21   https://www.usatoday.com/story/news/nation-now/2015/07/02/salvation-army-150th-anniversary/29596003/

22   https://www.wsj.com/articles/chick-fil-as-lean-menu-helps-chain-bulk-up-11557313200?mod=hp_lead_pos6

23   https://capitol.texas.gov/BillLookup/History.aspx?LegSess=86R&Bill=SB1978

24   https://triblive.com/sports/trans-woman-cyclist-wins-gold-sets-record-at-world-championships/

25   https://www.foxnews.com/sports/transgender-cyclist-rachel-mckinnon

26   https://www.statesman.com/news/20190809/shade-of-it-all-austin-councilman-tells-lgbtq-critic-to-sashay-away

27   statesman.com/news/20191029/austin-school-district-approves-revised-sex-ed-curriculum

28   https://txvalues.org/2019/10/29/austin-isd-adopts-radical-sex-education-opens-government-up-to-legal-attacks/

29   statesman.com/news/20191029/austin-school-district-approves-revised-sex-ed-curriculum

30   https://www.pewresearch.org/fact-tank/2017/02/15/u-s-students-internationally-math-science/

31   https://www.huffpost.com/entry/wage-gap_b_2073804

32   https://www.edweek.org/ew/articles/2017/08/15/the-na-tions-teaching-force-is-still-mostly.html

33   http://news.mit.edu/2016/why-do-women-leave-engineer-ing-0615

34   https://www.bls.gov/oes/current/oes_nat.htm#00-0000

35   http://www.austintexas.gov/sites/default/files/files/Auditor/Audit_Reports/Fleet_PM_Light_Duty__May_2017_.pdf

36   http://www.austintexas.gov/sites/default/files/files/Auditor/Audit_Reports/Matched_Savings_Account_Program__Janu-ary_2018_.pdf

37   http://www.austintexas.gov/sites/default/files/files/Au-ditor/Audit_Reports/Workforce_Development__Decem-ber_2017_.pdf

Chapter 4

38   Pam's name has been changed to protect her privacy.

39   https://www.forbes.com/sites/kathycaprino/2016/05/12/how-decision-making-is-different-between-men-and-wom-en-and-why-it-matters-in-business/#ce4cc264dcdf

40   https://www.nytimes.com/2016/10/25/upshot/the-problem-for-women-is-not-winning-its-deciding-to-run.html

41   https://www.theatlantic.com/magazine/archive/2014/05/the-confidence-gap/359815/

42   https://www.npr.org/2014/05/05/309832898/best-way-to-get-women-to-run-for-office-ask-repeatedly

Chapter 5

43   https://www.pewsocialtrends.org/2018/09/20/wom-en-and-leadership-2018/

44   https://fivethirtyeight.com/features/why-young-women-might-get-more-women-elected/

45   https://cawp.rutgers.edu/congressional-candidates-summa-ry-2018

46   https://www.vox.com/2018/11/6/18019234/women-re-cord-breaking-midterms

47   https://www.opensecrets.org/orgs/summary.php?id=D000000113&cycle=2018

48 https://www.influencewatch.org/political-party/run-for-something/

49 https://www.reformaustin.org/2019/10/23/hear-us-roar-how-women-are-reshaping-texas-politics/?fbclid=IwAR0E-0nLKoyJ93ZUM6_talVYpm8pchOl06BkI4yP-pz3A_xFff_hKd7nIItw

50 https://www.nytimes.com/2019/02/23/us/politics/justice-democrats-ocasio-cortez.html

51 Knock Down the House, Netflix Documentary.

52 https://www.pewforum.org/religious-landscape-study/state/alabama/views-about-abortion/

53 https://www.usatoday.com/story/news/nation/2019/05/15/alabama-abortion-law-american-views-abortion-poll-pro-life-pro-choice-republicans-catholic-heartbeat/3678315002/

54 https://www.huffpost.com/entry/leticia-van-de-putte_n_3500497

Chapter 6

55 https://news.gallup.com/poll/101905/gallup-poll.aspx

56 https://news.gallup.com/poll/1600/congress-public.aspx

57 https://www.dallasnews.com/news/politics/2019/05/03/abcs-20-20-features-dallas-woman-who-found-out-her-mothers-fertility-doctor-is-her-father/

58 https://chamberbusinessnews.com/2018/09/06/get-to-know-congresswoman-debbie-lesko/

59 https://www.thepolicycircle.org/

60 https://gov.texas.gov/organization/appointments

61 https://www.cnn.com/2016/04/25/politics/republican-delegate/index.html

62 https://www.c-span.org/video/?190221-1/qa-laura-ingraham

Chapter 8

63 https://www.forbes.com/sites/johnkartch/2016/05/08/austins-regulatory-regime-drives-uber-and-lyft-out-of-town/#1861c0bd110a

64 https://www.bizjournals.com/austin/blog/techflash/2016/01/austin-mayors-11th-hour-proposal-still-rankles.html

65 https://www.statesman.com/NEWS/20160915/Austin-to-
    vote-on-ride-hailing-law-May-7

66 https://www.kvue.com/article/news/local/lyft-uber-resume-
    service-in-austin/269-442904331

67 https://www.vox.com/the-highlight/2019/9/6/20851575/
    uber-lyft-drivers-austin-regulation-rideshare

9 781951 503048